VOGUE® KNITTING
Shawls & Wraps

VOGUE® KNITTING
Shawls & Wraps

the editors of Vogue Knitting Magazine

sixth&spring books

Sixth&Spring Books
233 Spring Street
New York, NY 10013

Book Division Manager
WENDY WILLIAMS

Technical Editor
CARLA SCOTT

Senior Editor
MICHELLE BREDESON

Yarn Editor
TANIS GRAY

Art Director
DIANE LAMPHRON

Copy Editor
KRISTINA SIGLER

Book Designer
JANEEN BELLAFIORE

Editorial Assistant
MIRLANDE JEANLOUIS

Vice President, Publisher
TRISHA MALCOLM

Production Manager
DAVID JOINNIDES

Creative Director
JOE VIOR

President
ART JOINNIDES

Library of Congress Control Number: 2009927135
ISBN: 978-1-933027-84-5

Manufactured in China

1 3 5 7 9 10 8 6 4 2

Contents

p. 22

p. 52

p. 82

p. 120

The Best
of the
Best

Why are shawls such perennially popular items to knit? I can't speak for all knitters, but I can tell you why I love shawls.

A shawl is the ultimate accessory. It is both an aesthetic statement and the most practical of garments. A dramatic wrap can provide the showstopping final touch to an elegant evening gown while keeping those bare shoulders warm. And nothing is more comforting to slip on than an oversized shawl knit with thick, soft yarns. Working in an office that is not always perfectly temperature-controlled, I can really appreciate the virtues of a cozy wrap. (In fact, we even have a box labeled "Office Shawls for Chilly People"!)

Shawls are accessible to all knitters, no matter their skill level or area of interest. Favorites of newer knitters who are stuck in a rut knitting scarf after scarf and want to branch out, shawls and wraps are also beloved by more advanced stitchers. Most shawls require little construction, making them accessible to beginners, but they are also the perfect canvas on which to play with color or to lose yourself in an intricate lace pattern. Most shawls (including the ones in this book) are one size fits all, so they make perfect gifts. And if you love to knit, but don't love lots of complicated finishing, shawls are for you.

I am thrilled to bring you *Vogue Knitting Shawls and Wraps*. This compilation of the best of the best shawl designs from our magazine is packed with gorgeous garments to knit and to wear. The issues of *Vogue Knitting* that feature shawls have been some of our most popular ever, and it's easy to see why. No matter the season or occasion, you'll find the perfect wrap to complete your wardrobe—from glamorous shawls that sparkle with beads and metallic yarns to gossamer-thin lace shawls to plush and comfy wraps that warm up the chilliest day (or office!). Many of today's top knitwear designers are represented here, and knitters of all styles and skill levels will find something to inspire their own creativity.

Trisha Malcolm
Editor in Chief, *Vogue Knitting*

Light&

Whisper-thin shawls knit with
exquisite yarns in intricate
lace patterns are the epitome
of graceful beauty.

Lacy

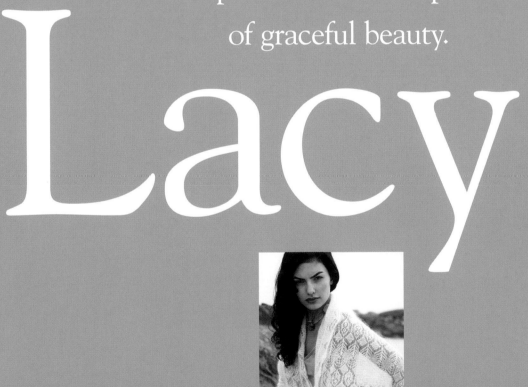

KNITTED MEASUREMENTS

Approx 40" x 40"/101.5cm x 101.5cm

MATERIALS
Original Yarns

3 3oz/85g hanks (each approx 262yd/240m) of Fiesta Yarns *Gelato* (rayon) in alaska (4)

3 2oz/57g hanks (each approx 310yd/283m) of *Heaven* (kid mohair/wool/nylon) in alaska (4)

Substitute Yarns

3 3oz/85g hanks (each approx 262yd/240m) of Fiesta Yarns *Gelato* (rayon) in alaska (4) (same as original yarn)

6 4oz/113g hanks (each approx 165yd/151m) of Fiesta Yarns *Insignia La Boheme* (rayon boucle/kid mohair/wool/nylon) in aegean blue (4)

One set (5) size 9 (5.5mm) double-pointed needles OR SIZE TO OBTAIN GAUGE

One each size 9 (5.5mm) circular needle, 24"/60cm and 60"/150cm lengths

Stitch markers

GAUGE

18 sts and 24 rnds = 4"/10cm over St st using size 9 (5.5mm) needles and *Gelato*.
TAKE TIME TO CHECK GAUGE.

STITCH GLOSSARY
Double Twist Drop St

Insert RH needle into next st and wrap yarn around BOTH needles, then yo around RH needle and draw yo through double wraps, allowing both wrapped loops to fall off ends of needles. Do not pull tight or adjust tension until next rnd.

Double Twist Drop Yo

Without inserting needle into a stitch, wrap yarn around BOTH needles, then yo around RH needle and draw yo through double wraps, allowing both wrapped loops to fall off ends of needles. Do not pull tight or adjust tension until next rnd.

4-st Picot Bind-off

*[K2tog tbl, sl st back to LH needle] 4 times, [k1, sl st back to LH needle] 3 times; rep from * around.

SHAWL

With dpn and *Gelato,* cast on 6 sts.

Next row Knit into the front and back of each st— 12 sts. Distribute sts evenly over 4 needles, place marker and join for knitting in the round. Inc as follows, changing to shorter circular needle, then to longer circular needle when sts no longer comfortably fit.

Rnd 1 Rep rnd 1 of chart A four times around, placing a marker every 3 sts to mark the 4 sections of the shawl. Work in this way through rnd 9 of chart A, isolating the center st of each rep by placing a contrasting marker on either side on last rnd—68 sts (17 sts each section).

Beg first dropped st section

Next rnd With *Heaven,* [work rnd 1 of chart B over first 2 sts, work rnd 1 of chart C to last 2 sts before section marker, work rnd 1 of chart D over

Squares and Stripes Lace Shawl

Annie Modesitt's sea-shaded shawl is knit circularly from the inside out in sections of lace surrounded by squares of dropped stitches.

CHART A

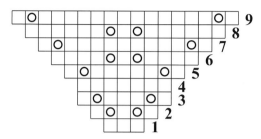

CHART D C **CHART B**

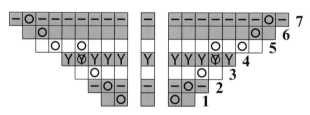

CHART G **CHART F** **CHART E**

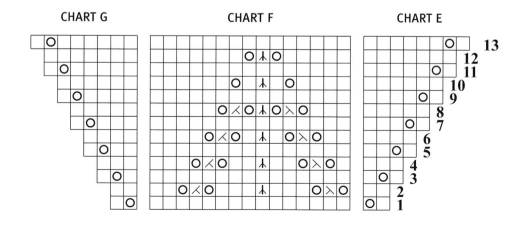

STITCH KEY

☐	k on RS, p on WS
—	p on RS, k on WS
Ⓞ	yo
⋏	s2kp
⟍	ssk on RS, p2tog on WS
⟋	k2tog on RS, ssp tbl on WS
Y̆	double twist drop, yarn over
Y	double twist drop stitch

COLOR KEY

☐	Gelato
▓	Heaven

last 2 sts] 4 times. Work in this way through rnd 7 of charts—132 sts (33 sts each section).

Beg first lace section

Next rnd With *Gelato,* [work rnd 1 chart E over first 2 sts, work rnd 1 of chart F to center st, sl center st, work rnd 1 of chart F to last 2 sts before section marker, work rnd 1 of chart G over last 2 sts] 4 times. Work in this way through rnd 13 of charts—188 sts (47 sts each section).

Beg second dropped st section

Next rnd With *Heaven,* [work rnd 1 of chart B over first 2 sts, work rnd 1 of chart C to last 2 sts before section marker, work rnd 1 of chart D over last 2 sts] 4 times. Work in this way through rnd 7 of charts—252 sts (63 sts each section).

Beg second lace section

Next rnd With *Gelato,* [work rnd 1 chart E over first 2 sts, rep rnd 1 of chart F twice to center st, sl center st, rep rnd 1 of chart F twice to last 2 sts before section marker, work rnd 1 of chart G over last 2 sts] 4 times. Work in this way through rnd 13 of charts   308 sts (77 sts each section).

Beg third dropped st section

Next rnd With *Heaven,* [work rnd 1 of chart B over first 2 sts, work rnd 1 of chart C to last 2 sts before section marker, work rnd 1 of chart D over last 2 sts] 4 times. Work in this way through rnd 7 of charts—372 sts (93 sts each section).

Beg third lace section

Next rnd With *Gelato,* [work rnd 1 chart E over first 2 sts, rep rnd 1 of chart F three times to center st, sl center st, rep rnd 1 of chart F three times to last 2 sts before section marker, work rnd 1 of chart G over last 2 sts] 4 times. Work in this way through rnd 13 of charts—428 sts (107 sts each section).

Beg fourth dropped st section

Next rnd With *Heaven,* [work rnd 1 of chart B over first 2 sts, work rnd 1 of chart C to last 2 sts before section marker, work rnd 1 of chart D over last 2 sts] 4 times. Work in this way through rnd 7 of charts—492 sts (123 sts each section).

Beg fourth lace section

Next rnd With *Gelato,* [work rnd 1 chart E over first 2 sts, rep rnd 1 of chart F four times to center st, sl center st, rep rnd 1 of chart F four times to last 2 sts before section marker, work rnd 1 of chart G over last 2 sts] 4 times. Work in this way through rnd 13 of charts—548 sts (137 sts each section).

Edging

Work 6 rnds in garter st, cont to inc 1 st before and after each corner marker each rnd—596 sts (149 sts each section). Work 4-st picot bind-off around edge.

FINISHING

Block to measurements. ✛

■■■■
KNITTED MEASUREMENTS

80" x 43"/201cm x 109cm

MATERIALS

Original Yarn

3 1¾oz/50g balls (each approx 385yd/350m) of S. Charles Collezione/Tahki•Stacy Charles, Inc. *Cashmere 7000* (cashmere) in #712104 dark teal (1)

Substitute Yarn

3 2oz/55g hanks (each approx 400yd/367m) of Jade Sapphire Exotic Fibres *Mongolian Cashmere 2-Ply* (Mongolian cashmere) in #44 deep denim (1)

One size 7 (4.5mm) circular needle, 24"/60cm length OR SIZE TO OBTAIN GAUGE

One 1mm beading crochet hook

1,000 size 6.0 glass beads

GAUGE

13 sts and 23 rows = 4"/10cm over chart pat.
TAKE TIME TO CHECK GAUGE.

NOTES

1) Only RS rows are shown on chart. Shawl is worked on RS rows as foll: K2, work chart pat to center st, k1 for center st, work chart pat to last 2 sts, k2.

2) Work WS rows as foll: K2, p to last 2 sts, k2.

STITCH GLOSSARY

Add Bead (AB)

Slip bead on to shank of beading crochet hook. With hook facing you, sl next st from LH needle onto crochet hook. Sl bead onto st. Sl st back onto LH needle and knit.

Diamond Motif Shawl

Iridescent beads emphasize the graphic nature of Karen Joan Raz's diamond motif triangle shawl.

3 to 2 Dec

Sl 1 knitwise, k2, pass sl st over the k2. One st has been decreased.

SHAWL

Cast on 5 sts. Knit 1 row.

Beg chart

Row 1 (RS) K2, yo for chart row 1, k1 for center st, yo for chart row 1, k2 —7 sts.

Row 2 (WS) K2, purl to last 2 sts, k2.

Row 3 K2, work chart row 3, k1, work chart row 3, k2—11 sts.

Row 4 K2, purl to last 2 sts, k2. Cont to work in this way through row 40—83 sts.

Row 41 K2, *beg with first st and work across chart row to beg of rep, work 30-st rep, work across to end of chart*, k1, work from * to * once more, k2. Work in this way through row 70—143 sts.

Row 71 K2, *beg with first st and work across chart row to beg of rep, work 30-st rep twice, work across to end of chart*, k1, work from * to * once more, k2. Work in this way through row 100—203 sts.

Row 101 K2, *beg with first st and work across chart row to beg of rep, work 30-st rep 3 times, work across to end of chart*, k1, work from * to * once more, k2. Work in this way through row 130—263 sts.

Row 131 K2, *beg with first st and work across

chart row to beg of rep, work 30-st rep 4 times, work across to end of chart*, k1, work from * to * once more, k2. Work in this way through row 160 — 323 sts.

Row 161 K2, *beg with first st and work across chart row to beg of rep, work 30-st rep 4 times, work across to end of chart*, k1, work from * to * once more, k2. Work in this way through row 186 — 375 sts. Bind off as foll: *K1, ssk, sl those 2 sts to LH needle; rep from * until 2 sts rem, ssk, fasten off last st.

FINISHING

Block shawl to measurements. ✢

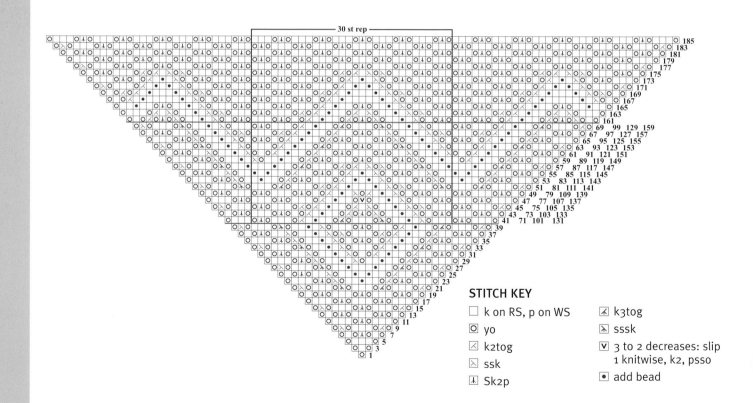

STITCH KEY

☐ k on RS, p on WS
◯ yo
╱ k2tog
╲ ssk
⅄ Sk2p

◿ k3tog
◺ sssk
V 3 to 2 decreases: slip 1 knitwise, k2, psso
• add bead

Spiderweb and Diamond Lace Shawl

Shirley Paden's lovely lacy shawl features a diamond scallop edging and a "spiderweb-and-diamond" pattern that mimics nature at its most delicate.

KNITTED MEASUREMENTS

Approx 69"/175cm wide by 26"/66cm long

MATERIALS

5 .88oz/25g balls (each approx 269yd/245m) of Filatura Di Crosa/Tahki•Stacy Charles, Inc. *Baby Kid Extra* (super kid mohair/nylon) in #310 off white (**1**)

One pair size 6 (4mm) needles OR SIZE TO OBTAIN GAUGE

One size 8 needle (5mm) for cast-on only

Stitch markers and holders

GAUGES

22 sts and 31 rows = 4"/10cm over garter st using size 6 (4mm) needles.

49 sts = 9"/23cm and 72 rows = 10½"/26.5cm (when steam blocked) over webs, spiders & diamonds pat.

TAKE TIME TO CHECK GAUGES.

NOTE

This shawl is made in 4 parts as foll: #1 & #2 The center section is composed of two identical halves that are grafted tog at the center. #3 The collar is made separately then seamed to the center of the top edge. Place the center of the collar at the grafted row. #4 The edging is worked separately, then sewn around the center section and collar beginning and ending at the center of the collar. The beg and end of the edging are then seamed together.

WEBS, SPIDERS & DIAMONDS

(multiple of 12 sts + 13 + 2 selvage sts)

NOTE 13 plus ("+") sts worked as foll:

RS rows 6 sts at beg, 7 sts at end

WS rows 7 sts at beg, 6 sts at end

Selvage st Worked in garter st (k every row).

On rows 16–20 and on row 30 the pattern moves as foll:

On rows 16, 18, 20 & 30 the reps slide forward = one st is borrowed from the upcoming rep until the last rep. Markers must be moved forward 1 st. On Rows 17 and 19 the reps slide back = there is one extra st at the end of each rep until the last rep. Markers must be moved back 1 st.

Row 1 (RS) 1 selvage st, k2tog, yo, k4, *k5, yo, SK2P, yo, k4; rep from *, end k5, yo, k2tog, 1 selvage st.

Row 2 1 selvage st, k1, k2tog, yo, k4, *k3, yo, k2tog, k1, k2tog, yo, k4; rep from *, end, k3, yo, k2tog, k1, 1 selvage st.

Row 3 1 selvage st, [k2tog, yo] twice, k2, *k3, yo, k2tog, yo, SK2P, yo, k2tog, yo, k2; rep from *, end k3, [yo, k2tog] twice, 1 selvage st.

Row 4 1 selvage st, k1, [k2tog, yo] twice, k2, *k1, [yo, k2tog] twice, k1, [k2tog, yo] twice, k2; rep from *, end k1, [yo, k2tog] twice, k1, 1 selvage st.

Row 5 1 selvage st, [k2tog, yo] 3 times, *k1, [yo, k2tog] twice, yo, SK2P, yo, [k2tog, yo] twice; rep from *, end k1, [yo, k2tog] 3 times, 1 selvage st.

Row 6 1 selvage st, k1, [k2tog, yo] 3 times, *k1, [yo, k2tog] twice, k1, [k2tog, yo] 3 times; rep from *, end k1, [yo, k2tog] twice, k1, 1 selvage st.

Row 7 1 selvage st, [k2tog, yo] 3 times, *k1, [yo, k2tog] twice, yo, SK2P, yo, [k2tog, yo] twice; rep from *, end k1, [yo, k2tog] 3 times, 1 selvage st.

Row 8 1 selvage st, k1, [k2tog, yo] twice, k2, *k1, [yo, k2tog] twice, k1, [k2tog, yo] twice, k2; rep from *, end k1, [yo, k2tog] twice, k1, 1 selvage st.

Row 9 1 selvage st, [k2tog, yo] twice, k2, *k3, yo, k2tog, yo, SK2P, yo, k2tog, yo, k2; rep from *, end k3, [yo, k2tog] twice, 1 selvage st.

Row 10 1 selvage st, k1, k2tog, yo, k4, *k3, yo, k2tog, k1, k2tog, yo, k4; rep from *, end k3, yo, k2tog, k1, 1 selvage st.

Row 11 1 selvage st, k2tog, yo, k4, *k5, yo, SK2P, yo, k4; rep from *, end k5, yo, k2tog, 1 selvage st.

Row 12 1 selvage st k1, yo, k2tog, k4, *k3, k2tog, yo, k1, yo, k2tog, k4; rep from *, end k3, k2tog, yo, k1, 1 selvage st.

Row 13 1 selvage st, k2, yo, k2tog, k2, *k3, k2tog, yo, k3, yo, k2tog, k2; rep from *, end k3, k2tog, yo, k2, 1 selvage st.

Row 14 1 selvage st, k3, yo, k2tog, k2, *k1, k2tog, yo, k5, yo, k2tog, k2; rep from *, end k1, k2tog, yo, k3, 1 selvage st.

Row 15 1 selvage st, [k1, yo, k2tog] twice, *[k1, k2tog, yo] twice, k1, yo, k2tog, k1, yo, k2tog; rep from *, end [k1, k2tog, yo] twice, k1, 1 selvage st.

Row 16 1 selvage st, k2, yo, k2tog, k1, yo, SK2P, *yo, k1, k2tog, yo, k3, yo, k2tog, k1, yo, SK2P; rep from *, end, yo, k1, k2tog, yo, k2, 1 selvage st.

Row 17 1 selvage st, k1, k2tog, yo, k2, yo, *SK2P, yo, k2, yo, k2tog, yo, SK2P, yo, k2, yo; rep from *, end SK2P, yo, k2, yo, k2tog, k1, 1 selvage st.

Row 18 1 selvage st, k2tog, yo, k3, yo, SK2P, *yo, k3, yo, SK2P, yo, k3, yo, SK2P; rep from *, end yo, k3, yo, k2tog, 1 selvage st.

Row 19 1 selvage st, k1, yo, k2tog, k2, yo, *SK2P, yo, k2, k2tog, yo, k1, yo, k2tog, k2, yo; rep from *, end SK2P, yo, k2, k2tog, yo, k1, 1 selvage st.

Row 20 1 selvage st, k2, yo, k2tog, k1, yo, SK2P, *yo, k1, k2tog, yo, k3, yo, k2tog, k1, yo, SK2P; rep from *, end yo, k1, k2tog, yo, k2, 1 selvage st.

Row 21 1 selvage st, [k1, k2tog, yo] twice, *[k1, yo, k2tog] twice, yo, SK2P, yo, k1, k2tog, yo; rep from *, end [k1, yo, k2tog] twice, k1, 1 selvage st.

Row 22 1 selvage st, k2tog, yo, k1, k2tog, yo, k2, *k1, yo, k2tog, k1, yo, SK2P, yo, k1, k2tog, yo, k2; rep from *, end [k1, yo, k2tog] twice, 1 selvage st.

Row 23 1 selvage st, k2, k2tog, yo, k2, *k3, yo, k2tog, k3, k2tog, yo, k2; rep from *, end k3, yo, k2tog, k2, 1 selvage st.

Row 24 1 selvage st, k1, k2tog, yo, k4, *k3, yo, k2tog, k1, k2tog, yo, k4; rep from *, end k3, yo, k2tog, k1, 1 selvage st.

Row 25 1 selvage st, k2tog, yo, k4, *k5, yo, SK2P, yo, k4; rep from *, end k5, yo, k2tog, 1 selvage st.

Row 26 1 selvage st, k1, yo, k2tog, k4, *k3, k2tog, yo, k1, yo, k2tog, k4; rep from *, end k3, k2tog, yo, k1, 1 selvage st.

Row 27 1 selvage st, k2, yo, k2tog, k2, *k3, k2tog, yo, k3, yo, k2tog, k2; rep from *, end k3, k2tog, yo, k2, 1 selvage st.

Row 28 1 selvage st, k1, [yo, k2tog] twice, k2, *k1, [k2tog, yo] twice, k1, [yo, k2tog] twice, k2; rep from *, end k1, [k2tog, yo] twice, k1, 1 selvage st.

Row 29 1 selvage st, k2, [yo, k2tog] twice, *k1, [k2tog, yo] twice, k3, [yo, k2tog] twice; rep from *, end k1, [k2tog, yo] twice, k2, 1 selvage st.

Row 30 1 selvage st, k1, [yo, k2tog] twice, yo, SK2P, *[yo, k2tog] twice; yo, k1, yo, [k2tog, yo] twice, SK2P; rep from *, end [yo, k2tog] twice, yo, k1, 1 selvage st.

Row 31 1 selvage st, k2, [yo, k2tog] twice, *k1, [k2tog, yo] twice, k3, [yo, k2tog] twice; rep from *, end k1, [k2tog, yo] twice, k2, 1 selvage st.

Row 32 1 selvage st, k1, [yo, k2tog] twice, k2, *k1, [k2tog, yo] twice, k1, [yo, k2tog] twice, k2; rep from *, end k1, [k2tog, yo] twice, k1, 1 selvage st.

Row 33 1 selvage st, k2, yo, k2tog, k2, *k3, k2tog, yo, k3, yo, k2tog, k2; rep from *, end k3, k2tog, yo, k2, 1 selvage st.

Row 34 1 selvage st, k1, yo, k2tog, k4, *k3, k2tog, yo, k1, yo, k2tog, k4; rep from *, end k3, k2tog, yo, k1, 1 selvage st.

Row 35 1 selvage st, yo, k2tog, k4, *k5, k2tog, yo, k5; rep from *, end k5, k2tog, yo, 1 selvage st.

Row 36 Knit.

LACE & DIAMONDS EDGING

(10-st cast-on and 14-row rep)

NOTE On WS rows make first stitch yarn overs by working the 2nd (knit) sts with the yarn held in front of the needle.

Row 1 K1, k2tog, yo, k3 [yo, k2tog] twice—10 sts (3 + 7).

Row 2 Yo, k1, yo, k2tog, yo, k7—12 sts (9 + 3).

Row 3 k1, k2tog, yo, k5 [yo, k2tog] twice—12 sts (3 + 9).

Row 4 Yo, k1, yo, k2tog, yo, k9—14 sts (11 + 3).

Row 5 K1, k2tog, yo, K7, [yo, k2tog] twice—14 sts (3 + 11).

Row 6 Yo, k1, yo, k2tog, yo, k11—16 sts (13 + 3).

Row 7 K1, k2tog, yo, k9 [yo, k2tog] twice—16 sts (3 + 13).

Row 8 Yo, [k2tog, yo] twice, k2tog, k10—16 sts (13 + 3).

Row 9 K1, k2tog, yo, k6, [k2tog, yo] twice, k3tog—14 sts (3 + 11).

Row 10 Yo, [k2tog, yo] twice, k2tog, k8—14 sts (11 + 3).

Row 11 K1, k2tog, yo, k4 [k2tog, yo] twice, k3tog—12 sts (3 + 9).

Row 12 Yo, [k2tog, yo]twice, k2tog, k6—12 sts (9 + 3).

Row 13 K1, k2tog, yo, k2 [k2tog, yo] twice, k3tog—10 sts (3 + 7).

Row 14 Yo, [k2tog, yo] twice, k2tog, k4—10 sts (7 +3).

Sloped Bind-Off

Used on the collar. Do not work the last st on the row before the bind off, turn, slip the first st from the LH needle purlwise, then bind the leftover st off over the slipped st. This technique is used only on the first bind-off on the row.

SHAWL

Center

With size 8 (5mm) needle cast on 111 sts using the long-tail cast-on. Change to size 6 (4mm) needles. Set up markers as foll: 8 pat reps of 12 sts + 13 "plus" sts + 2 selvage sts. Work even on these 111 sts for 5 row reps of 36 rows. On the 6th rep work 35 rows, then leave all sts on a holder. Work a 2nd piece repeating from * to * then work 6 full 36-row reps. Place pieces side by side and graft at center.

Shawl collar

NOTE All increases and decreases are made at the same edge of the collar.

With size 6 (4mm) needle cast on 1 st. On Row 1 (RS) inc 1 st by knitting into the front and back of the st.

Shape right collar

Working in garter st, inc 1 st at the end of every foll 4th RS row 24 times—25 sts on needle. Piece should measure 12"/30.5cm long and 4½"/11.5cm wide.

Back neck

Work even on these 25 sts for 7"/17.5cm. Piece should measure 19"/48cm long and end with a RS row. Do not work the last st.

Shape left collar

Using the Sloped Bind-Off decrease technique, bind off 1 st at the beg of the next WS row, then at the beg of every foll 4th WS row 24 times—1 st rem. Cut yarn and pull it through the st. Piece should measure 31"/78.5cm long.

Edging

With size 8 (5mm) needle, using the long-tail cast-on technique, cast on 10 sts. Change to size 6 (4mm) needles and work the 14-row Lace & Diamonds edging pattern until piece is long enough to completely border the shawl and collar—approx 80 complete reps.

FINISHING

Block all pieces to measurements. Baste edging in place, gathering two edging reps around each corner so that edging lies flat. With RS of center section facing, sew collar to center of top lengthwise edge using a whip st sewing technique. Sew edging around the entire center section beg and end at the center of the shawl collar. Use the edge-to-edge seaming technique so that there is a barely visible seam on the reverse side. Work as foll: Beg sewing edging to right collar on the outside side as the collar will turn backward. At the end of the collar, reverse the sewing to the inside around the center of the shawl with the exception of the corners.

Work corners

On center section beg 7 garter edge bumps before corner and 7 bumps after, pull yarn to outside and use the mattress stitch weaving technique on the right side (seam will turn to inside). Work 2 sts of edging for 1 st of center section. Working this way will create small gathers at the corners to enable the edging to lie flat as it turns around the corner when it is lightly steamed. After each corner is seamed, pull the yarn back to the inside and continue using the edge-to-edge seaming technique. At the end pull yarn to outside and reverse the seaming on the left collar. Seam both ends of the edging tog at the center collar using mattress stitch. Steam seams and corners. ✦

Floral Lace Shawl

A top-down triangle shawl by
Susan Haviland opens up in
a contemporary lace pattern; the
petal edge is knit on afterward.

■■■■

KNITTED MEASUREMENTS

Top width 66"/167.5cm (after blocking)

Length 28"/71cm (after blocking)

MATERIALS

4 1¾oz/50g hanks (each approx 140yd/128m)
of Tilli Tomas *Fil de la Mer* (silk/seacell) in
coral **④**

Size 5 (3.75mm) circular needle, 24" or 29"
(60cm or 75cm) length OR SIZE TO OBTAIN
GAUGE

Two size 5 (3.75mm) dpn for edging

Rubber band or point protector, blocking pins for
finishing and stitch marker

GAUGE

20 sts and 28 rows to 4"/10cm over St st using
size 5 (3.75mm) needles (before blocking).
TAKE TIME TO CHECK GAUGE.

NOTE

You can work from written instructions or from
chart.

STITCH GLOSSARY

RE inc (Right edge increase) K2, yo—3 sts.

LE inc (Left edge increase) Yo, k2—3 sts.

C inc (Center Increase) Yo, k1, yo—3 sts.

LACE PATTERN (multiple of 8 sts plus 1)

Rows 1 and 3 (RS) Knit.

Row 2 and all WS rows Purl.

Rows 5 and 7 *K1, yo, k2, S2KP, k2, yo; rep from
*, end k1.

Row 8 Purl. Rep rows 1–8 for lace pat.

EDGING PATTERN

Cast on 5 sts.

Row 1 (RS) Sl 1, k1, k2tog, M1, k1.

Row 2 K1, (k1, p1, k1, p1, k1) in next st, M1, k2tog,
k last edging st and next shawl st tog.

Rows 3, 5 and 7 Sl 1, k1, M1, k2 tog, k5.

Rows 4 and 6 K6, M1, k2tog, k last edging st and
next shawl st tog.

Row 8 Bind off 4 sts, K1, m1, k2tog, k last edging
st and next shawl st tog.

SHAWL

Beg at back neck, cast on 5 sts. Knit 1 row on WS.

Row 1 K2, yo, k1 (center st), yo, k2—7 sts. Place
st marker on center st. Move this marker every
row, keeping on the center stitch.

Row 2 and all WS rows K2, p to last 2 sts, k2.

Row 3 K2, yo (for RE inc), k1; yo, k1, yo (for C inc),
k1; yo, k2 (for LE inc)—11 sts.

Row 5 RE inc, k3, C inc, k3, LE inc—15 sts.

Row 7 RE inc, k5, yo, k1, yo, k5, LE inc—19 sts.

Row 9 RE inc, k7, C inc, k7, LE inc—23 sts.

Row 11 RE inc, *k1, yo, k2, S2KP, k2, yo, k1, (row
5 of lace pat)*; C inc; rep between *'s to last 2
sts, LE inc—27 sts.

Row 13 RE inc, *k2, yo, k2, S2KP, k2, yo, k2*; C
inc; rep between *'s to last 2 sts, LE inc—31 sts.

Row 15 RE inc, k to center st, C inc, k to last 2 sts,
LE inc—35 sts.

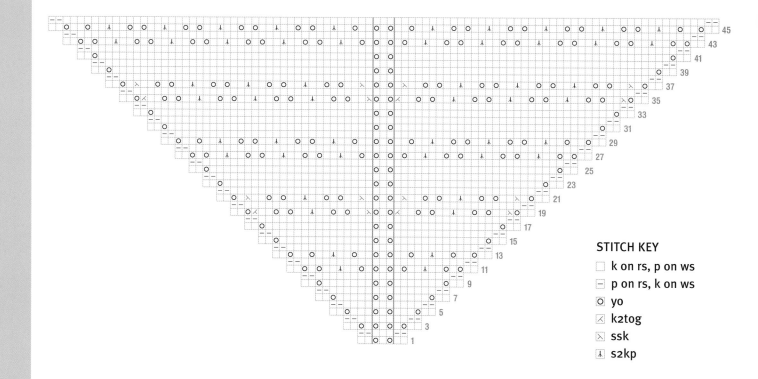

45
43
41
39
37
35
33
31
29
27
25
23
21
19
17
15
13
11
9
7
5
3
1

STITCH KEY

☐ k on rs, p on ws

– p on rs, k on ws

O yo

⟋ k2tog

⟍ ssk

⅄ s2kp

Row 17 Rep row 15 —39 sts.

Row 19 RE inc, *ssk, k2, yo, [k1, yo, k2, S2KP, k2, yo], k1, yo, k2, k2 tog*; C inc; rep between *'s once, LE inc—43 sts.

Row 21 RE inc, *k1, ssk, k2, yo, [k1, yo, k2, S2KP, k2, yo], k1, yo, k2, ssk, k1*, C inc; rep between *'s once, LE inc—47 sts.

Row 23 Rep row 15 —51 sts.

Row 25 Rep row 15 —55 sts.

Row 27 RE inc, *[k1, yo, k2, S2KP, k2, yo] 3 times, k1*; C inc; rep between *'s once, LE inc—59 sts.

Row 29 RE inc, *k1, [k1, yo, k2, S2KP, k2, yo] 3 times, k2*, C inc; rep between *'s once, LE inc— 63 sts.

Row 31 Rep row 15 —67 sts.

Row 33 Rep row 15 —71 sts.

Row 35 RE inc, *ssk, k2, yo, [k1, yo, k2, S2KP, k2, yo] 3 times, k1, yo, k2, k2tog*; C inc; rep between *'s once, LE inc—75 sts.

Row 37 RE inc, *k1, ssk, k2, yo, [k1, yo, k2, S2KP, k2, yo] 3 times, k1, yo, k2, ssk, k1*, C inc; rep between *'s once, LE inc—79 sts.

Row 39 Rep row 15 —83 sts.

Row 41 Rep row 15 —87 sts.

Row 43 RE inc, *[k1, yo, k2, S2KP, k2, yo] 5 times, k1*; C inc; rep between *'s once, LE inc—91 sts.

Row 45 RE inc, *k1, [k1, yo, k2, S2KP, k2, yo] 5 times, k2*, C inc; rep between *'s once, LE inc— 95 sts.

Row 46 K2, p to last 2 sts, k2.

Cont to rep rows 31–46, increasing 4 sts every RS row into the pattern. The pattern multiples will increase by 2 every 16 rows.

Work until there are 255 sts on the needle, (127 on right side, 1 center st, 127 on left side). Purl next row on WS. Knit 1 row. Place a rubber band or protector at end of row to keep stitches in place as edging is worked.

Edging

Do not break yarn. Cast on 5 sts for edging. With dpn, knit 4 of the new sts, k the last st tog with the first st of shawl edge. Turn work to RS, and work row 1 of edging pattern. Cont to work until 31 reps of 8-row edging pat have been worked. You will be at bottom point of the shawl.

Next repeat Work rows 1 and 2, work last st of row 2 as k1, do not attach to shawl. Work rows 3 and 4, attaching to shawl at end of row 4. Work rows 5 and 6, do not attach. Work rows 7 and 8 attaching at end of row 8. Work rows 1 and 2 and do not attach. Attaching the even rows as usual, work the remaining rows of this repeat and cont to work edging up other side of shawl—64 edging repeats. Bind off the 5 rem edging sts.

FINISHING

Submerge the shawl in water. Gently squeeze out some water, roll the shawl in a large bath towel and press so water goes into the towel. Repeat with a second towel. Lay shawl flat on a sheet and spread out. Pin at edges of triangle first, then pin each edge scallop and across long top of shawl. The silk-blend yarn dries quickly. ✢

KNITTED MEASUREMENTS

Hexagon (point to point) 8"/20.5cm

Shawl 34½" x 32"/87.5cm x 81.5cm

MATERIALS

4 1¾oz/50g hanks (each approx 144yd/133m) of Berroco, Inc. *Ultra Alpaca Light* (superfine alpaca/Peruvian highland wool) in #4283 lavender mix (**3**)

One size 7 (4.5mm) circular needle, 16"/40cm length

OR SIZE TO OBTAIN GAUGE

One size F/5 (3.75mm) crochet hook

Stitch marker

Tapestry needle

GAUGE

1 hexagon = 8"/20.5cm after blocking.

TAKE TIME TO CHECK GAUGE.

HEXAGONS (make 15)

Cast on 96 sts. Place marker and join for knitting in the round. Rep chart 6 times around, working through rnd 20. Cut yarn with a 12"/30.5cm tail. Thread through 36 rem sts and cinch tightly to close.

FINISHING

Block hexagons lightly. Arrange hexagons according to placement diagram and join with crochet hook, holding WS tog, as foll:

To join along one edge Sc in first and 2nd sts, ch 7, skip 5, sc in next 2 sts, ch 7, skip 5, sc in last 2 sts.

To join along two or more edges Sc in first and 2nd sts, ch 7, skip 5, *sc in next 2 sts, ch 8, skip 6, sc in last st of hexagon, sc in first st of next hexagon, ch 8, skip 6; rep from *, end ch 7, skip 5, sc in last 2 sts.

To work outside edging Work same as joining two or more edges, and working at each outside point as foll: Sc in last 2 sts, ch 4, sc in first 2 sts. ✤

Medallion Wrap

Norah Gaughan employs her signature hexagons for an enchanting lavender wrap, knitting each motif separately and piecing them together in a half-circle.

HEXAGON PLACEMENT DIAGRAM

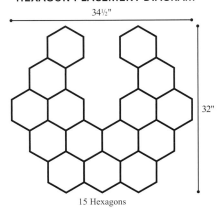

34½"

32"

15 Hexagons

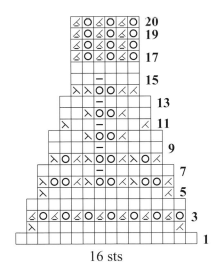

16 sts

STITCH KEY

☐	k on rs	⟋	skp
−	p on rs	⟍	p2tog
⟋	k2tog	O	yo

Trellis Lace Shawl

Worked in a delicate trellis pattern, this barely there stole by lace artisan Margaret Stove works for all climates and occasions.

KNITTED MEASUREMENTS

Approx 18" x 80"/45.5cm x 203cm

MATERIALS

1 8oz/227g ball (approx 2400yd/2195m) of Cherry Tree Hill *Merino Lace Weight* (merino wool) in undyed

One pair size 2 (2.5mm) needles OR SIZE TO OBTAIN GAUGE

Two size 2 (2.5mm) dpn

Stitch holder

GAUGE

36 sts and 44 rows = 4"/10cm over St st using size 2 (2.5mm) needles.

TAKE TIME TO CHECK GAUGE.

TRELLIS PATTERN (multiple of 15 sts plus 4)

Row 1 K4, *[yo, ssk] twice, yo, sl 2, k1, p2sso, [yo, k2tog] twice, yo, k1, p2, k1; rep from * to last 15 sts, [yo, ssk] twice, yo, sl 2, k1, p2sso, [yo, k2tog] twice, yo, k4.

Rows 2 and 4 K3, *p13, k2; rep from * to last 16 sts, p13, k3.

Row 3 K3, *[yo, ssk] 3 times, k1, [k2tog, yo] 3 times, p2; rep from * to last 16 sts, [yo, ssk] 3 times, k1, [k2tog, yo] 3 times, k3.

Rep rows 1–4 for trellis pat.

SHAWL (make 2 pieces)

**Cast on 154 sts. K 1 row.

Next 3 rows K2, *inc 1 st in next st, k5, sl 2, k1, p2sso, k5, inc 1 st in next st; rep from * to last 2 sts, k2. K 1 row.**

Beg trellis pat

Work 4 rows of trellis pat 6 times, end with row

3. Break yarn and sl sts to a holder.

Beg second layer

Rep from ** to **, then work 4 rows of trellis pat twice, end with row 3.

Attach layers

Next row With needles parallel, WS facing, and using 3rd needle, work row 4 of trellis pat, working sts tog from both needles. Cont on the one piece in trellis pat until piece measures 40"/101.5cm from beg, end with row 1 of pat. Place sts on a holder.

FINISHING

Graft the 2 pieces tog so that lace pat is in opposite directions. Steam lightly. ✛

Wavy Edge Lace Shawl

The lace interior of Cookie A's square shawl begins at the center and is surrounded by a fan border. Using a hand-dyed yarn creates a subtle but beautiful effect.

KNITTED MEASUREMENTS

48" x 48"/122cm x 122cm

MATERIALS

12 1¾oz/50g hanks (each approx 131yd/120m) of Colinette/Unique Kolours, Ltd. *Cadenza* (merino wool) in #119 alizarine ⑧

One set (5) size 8 (5mm) dpn OR SIZE TO OBTAIN GAUGE

One each size 8 (5mm) circular needle, 24"/60cm and 60"/150cm lengths

Stitch markers

GAUGE

24 sts and 25 rnds = 4"/10cm over pat st using size 8 (5mm) needles.

TAKE TIME TO CHECK GAUGE.

SHAWL

With dpn, cast on 8 sts. Place marker and join for knitting in the round.

Rnd 1 *Knit into the front and back of next st (kfb); rep from * to marker—16 sts.

Rnd 2 and all even rnds unless otherwise noted Knit.

Rnd 3 [Kfb, k2, kfb] 4 times—24 sts.

Rnd 5 [K1, k2tog, yo, k1, yo, ssk] 4 times.

Rnd 7 [K2, yo, k3, yo, k1] 4 times—32 sts.

Rnd 8 Place markers as foll: [k8, pm] 4 times.

Beg pat st

Rnd 9 [K2, yo, k1, yo, SK2P, [yo, k1] twice, sl marker (sl m)] 4 times—40 sts.

Rnd 11 [K2, yo, k3, yo, k1 tbl, yo, k3, yo, k1, sl m] 4 times—56 sts.

Rnds 12 and 14 Knit.

Rnd 13 [K2, yo, k1, *yo, SK2P; rep from * to 2 sts before marker, (yo, k1) twice, sl m] 4 times.

Rnd 15 [K2, *yo, k3, yo, k1 tbl; rep from * to 4 sts before marker, yo, k3, yo, k1, sl m] 4 times—80 sts. Rep rnds 12–15 twenty more times—560 sts.

Beg border chart

Rnd 96 [Work across row to rep, work 18-st rep 7 times, work to end row] 4 times. Work in this way through rnd 131 of chart.

Rnd 132 [Work across row to rep, work 18-st pat rep 9 times, work to end of row] 4 times. Work in this way through rnd 145 of chart. Bind off loosely.

FINISHING

Block to measurements. ✢

BORDER CHART

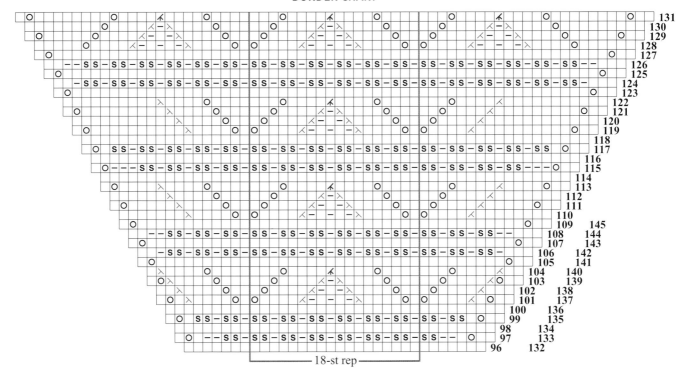

18-st rep

STITCH KEY

☐ k on rs

⊟ p on rs

⊡ yo

◿ k2tog on rs

◺ ssk on rs

⋏ k3 tog on rs

Ⓢ on rs, wyif, sl 1 st purlwise

Summer Lace Shawl

Maureen Egan Emlet's elegant shawl with exquisite lace border is summer's ultimate accessory. Once the easy lace pattern on the body is mastered, the edging is picked up and knit on. This a statement piece, sure to become an heirloom.

KNITTED MEASUREMENTS

74½" x 23½"/189.5cm x 59.5cm at widest points (including edging)

MATERIALS

Original Yarn

5 1¾oz/50g balls (each approx 119yd/110m) of GGH/Meunch Yarns *Mystik* (rayon) in #1 white 〔3〕

Substitute Yarn

7 2oz/57g hanks (each approx 88yd/80m) of Prism Yarns *Bolero* (rayon) in creme 〔4〕
One size 5 (3.75mm) circular needle, 29"/74cm long OR SIZE TO OBTAIN GAUGE
One dpn, any size under 5

GAUGE

18 sts and 32 rows = 4"/10cm over Chart I, using size 5 (3.75mm) needle.
TAKE TIME TO CHECK GAUGE.

NOTES

Work shawl decs 1 st in from each side edge, making adjustments to Chart I pat as necessary to maintain correct st count. Bind off when decreasing more than one st at a time. Shawl directions indicate the number of sts that should be decreased at each side on a given row.

STITCH GLOSSARY

P2tog tbl
P 2 sts tog through their back loops.
Ssk
Sl 2 sts knitwise, one at a time, to RH needle,

then insert LH needle into fronts of these 2 sts and k them tog.

SKP

Sl 1, k1, psso.

SK2P

Sl 1, k2tog, psso.

S2KP2

Sl 2 sts tog knitwise, k1, p2sso.

CHART I (multiple of 6 sts, plus 1)

Rows 1 and 3 (WS) Purl. **Row 2** K1, *yo, ssk, k1, k2tog, yo, k1; rep from * to end.

Row 4 K1, *k1, yo, S2KP2, yo, k2; rep from * to end.

Rep rows 1–4 for Chart I.

CHART II (begin on 19 sts)

NOTE Sl sts purlwise wyif.

Row 1 (RS) Sl 1, k3, [yo, p2tog] twice, k4, yo, ssk, [yo, p2tog] twice, k1.

Row 2 (WS) K1, [yo, p2tog] 3 times, k4, [yo, p2tog] twice, k4.

Row 3 Sl 1, k3, [yo, p2tog] twice, k3, k2tog, yo, k1, [yo, p2tog] twice, yo, [p1, k1] in last st.

Row 4 K1, yo, k2, [yo, p2tog] twice, k2, yo, p2tog, k2, [yo, p2tog] twice, k4.

Row 5 Sl 1, k3, [yo, p2tog] twice, k1, k2tog, yo, k3, [yo, p2tog] twice, yo, k3, [p1, k1] in last st. Turn. K1, yo, k2, yo, p2tog. Turn. Yo, p2tog, yo, k3, [p1, k1] in last st.

Row 6 Bind off 5 sts (1 st rem on RH needle), yo, p2tog, k1, [yo, p2tog] twice, k4, [yo, p2tog] 3 times, k4.

Row 7 Sl 1, k3, [yo, p2tog] twice, yo, ssk, k4, [yo, p2tog] twice, [p1, k1] in next st, yo, p2tog, yo, [p1, k1] in last st. *Turn. K3, yo, p2tog. Turn. Yo, p2tog, yo, k2, yo, [p1, k1] in last st.*

Row 8 Bind off 5 sts, yo, p2tog, yo, k2, [yo, p2tog] twice, k3, p2tog tbl, yo, k1, [yo, p2tog] twice, k4.

Row 9 Sl 1, k3, [yo, p2tog] twice, k2, yo, ssk, k2, [yo, p2tog] twice, k2, [p1, k1] in next st, yo, p2tog, yo, [p1, k1] in last st; rep between *'s of row 7.

Row 10 Bind off 5 sts, yo, p2tog, yo, k4, [yo, p2tog] twice, k1, p2tog tbl, yo, k3, [yo, p2tog] twice, k4.

Row 11 Sl 1, k3, [yo, p2tog] twice, k4, yo, ssk, [yo, p2tog] twice, k4, [p1, k1] in next st, yo, p2tog, yo, [p1, k1] in last st; rep between *'s of row 7.

Row 12 Bind off 5 sts, yo, p2tog, yo, k6, [yo, p2tog] 3 times, k4, [yo, p2tog] twice, k4.

Row 13 Sl 1, k3, [yo, p2tog] twice, k3, k2tog, yo, k1, [yo, p2tog] twice, k6, [p1, k1] in next st, yo, p2tog, yo, [p1, k1] in last st; rep between *'s of row 7.

Row 14 Bind off 5 sts, yo, p2tog, yo, k8, [yo, p2tog] twice, k2, yo, p2tog, k2, [yo, p2tog] twice, k4.

Row 15 Sl 1, k3, [yo, p2tog] twice, k1, k2tog, yo, k3, [yo, p2tog] twice, k8, [p1, k1] in next st, yo, p2tog, yo, [p1, k1] in last st; rep between *'s of row 7.

Row 16 Bind off 5 sts, yo, p2tog, yo, p3tog, k7, [yo, p2tog] twice, k4, [yo, p2tog] 3 times, k4.

Row 17 Sl 1, k3, [yo, p2tog] twice, yo, ssk, k4, [yo, p2tog] twice, k6, k2tog, k1, yo, p2tog, yo, [p1, k1] in last st; rep between *'s of row 7.

Row 18 Bind off 5 sts, yo, p2tog, yo, p3tog, k5, [yo, p2tog] twice, k3, p2tog tbl, yo, k1, [yo, p2tog] twice, k4.

Row 19 Sl 1, k3, [yo, p2tog] twice, k2, yo, ssk, k2, [yo, p2tog] twice, k4, k2tog, k1, yo, p2tog, yo, [p1, k1] in last st; rep between *'s of row 7.

Row 20 Bind off 5 sts, yo, p2tog, yo, p3tog, k3,

CHART II

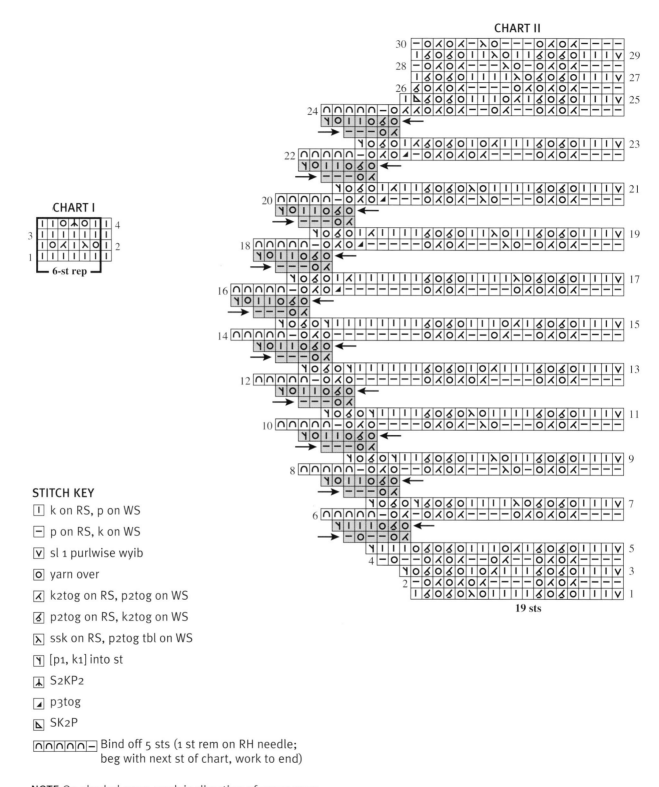

CHART I

6-st rep

STITCH KEY

- ☐ k on RS, p on WS
- ☐ p on RS, k on WS
- ☑ sl 1 purlwise wyib
- ☐ yarn over
- ☐ k2tog on RS, p2tog on WS
- ☐ p2tog on RS, k2tog on WS
- ☐ ssk on RS, p2tog tbl on WS
- ☐ [p1, k1] into st
- ☐ S2KP2
- ☐ p3tog
- ☐ SK2P

∩∩∩∩∩☐ Bind off 5 sts (1 st rem on RH needle; beg with next st of chart, work to end)

NOTE On shaded rows, work in direction of arrow over sts in shaded boxes only, turn, work next shaded row.

[yo, p2tog] twice, k1, p2tog tbl, yo, k3, [yo, p2tog] twice, k4.

Row 21 Sl 1, k3, [yo, p2tog] twice, k4, yo, ssk, [yo, p2tog] twice, k2, k2tog, k1, yo, p2tog, yo, [p1, k1] in last st; rep between *'s of row 7.

Row 22 Bind off 5 sts, yo, p2tog, yo, p3tog, k1, [yo, p2tog] 3 times, k4, [yo, p2tog] twice, k4.

Row 23 Sl 1, k3, [yo, p2tog] twice, k3, k2tog, yo, k1, [yo, p2tog] twice, k2tog, k1, yo, p2tog, yo, [p1, k1] in last st; rep between *'s of row 7.

Row 24 Bind off 5 sts, yo, [p2tog] twice, [yo, p2tog] twice, k2, yo, p2tog, k2, [yo, p2tog] twice, k4.

Row 25 Sl 1, k3, [yo, p2tog] twice, k1, k2tog, yo, k3, [yo, p2tog] twice, SK2P, k1.

Row 26 K2tog, [yo, p2tog] twice, k4, [yo, p2tog] 3 times, k4.

Row 27 Sl 1, k3, [yo, p2tog] twice, yo, ssk, k4, [yo, p2tog] twice, k1.

Row 28 K1, [yo, p2tog] twice, k3, p2tog tbl, yo, k1, [yo, p2tog] twice, k4.

Row 29 Sl 1, k3, [yo, p2tog] twice, k2, yo, ssk, k2, [yo, p2tog] twice, k1.

Row 30 K1, [yo, p2tog] twice, k1, p2tog tbl, yo, k3, [yo, p2tog] twice, k4.

Rep rows 1–30 for Chart II.

SHAWL

With circular needle, cast on 277 sts. K 6 rows. Work Chart I, AT SAME TIME, dec 1 st each side as foll: on 11th row, then foll 6th row once, 5th row once, 4th row once, then every 3rd row 10 times, every other row twice, [on next row, then on alternate row] 7 times, every row 11 times. Cont dec or binding off each side on every row as foll: [2 sts once, then 1 st once] 4 times, 1 st twice, [2 sts once, then 1 st once] 3 times, [3 sts once, then 1 st once] 5 times, [4 sts once, then 1 st once] twice, [5 sts once, then 1 st once] 3 times, 5 sts once (130 total chart rows). Bind off rem 43 sts.

Edging

With RS facing and garter st border at lower edge, tip up lower LH corner of shawl and with dpn pick up and p5 sts along WS of garter st border rows, leave yarn. With circular needle and separate skein, cast on 19 sts. **Next row (WS)** K18, then holding needles parallel, k last st on circular needle tog with first picked-up st on dpn. Turn. **Next row (RS)** Wyib, sl 1 st from dpn to circular needle, k2tog, k to end. K 3 more rows, joining sts as before on every row. Turn.

Beg Chart II

Next row (RS) Work row 1 of Chart II over 19 sts on circular needle. Measure around shawl and place a yarn marker every 4"/10cm (omitting garter st rows at end). With dpn and yarn left from picking up sts, pick up and p15 sts (from WS) between last row worked and next marker. Work chart row 2, k last st of chart tog with 1 st from dpn. Turn. Work chart row 3 (do not join sts). Cont working Chart II over sts on circular needle, knitting tog the last st of each WS row tog with 1 st on dpn. 30 rows of chart will be worked between each pair of markers. Work until 30 rows of chart have been worked 17 times, picking up 15 sts along edge for each 30-row rep of chart. Pick up and p 6 sts along garter rows. K 6 rows, joining edging to shawl on every row as before, binding off all sts on last row.

FINISHING

Dampen shawl and pin to size, placing 1 pin in each point around edging. Let dry completely. ✤

■■■■▶

KNITTED MEASUREMENTS

Approx 80"/203cm x 40"/101.5cm

MATERIALS

2 2oz/60g balls (each approx 825yd/754m) of Jade Sapphire Exotic Fibres *Lacey Lamb* (extrafine lambswool) in #304 periwinkle (**1**)

550 size 6.0 glass beads (approx 32g), silver lined crystal with rainbow finish

One size 5 (3.75mm) 24"/60cm circular needle OR SIZE TO OBTAIN GAUGE

One 1mm beading crochet hook

One extra needle for 3 needle bind-off

GAUGE

18 sts and 36 rows to 4"/10cm over lace pattern, blocked, using size 5 (3.75mm) needles.
TAKE TIME TO CHECK GAUGE.

NOTE

Beads are added on a wrong side row.

STITCH GLOSSARY

Add Bead

Slip bead onto shank of crochet hook. With hook facing you, slip next st from LH needle onto crochet hook. Hold taut. Slip bead onto st. Slip st back to LH needle and purl.

SHAWL

Cast on 5 sts and knit one row on WS.

Begin chart

Row 1 (RS) K2, yo for chart row 1, k1 for center st, yo for chart row 1, k2—7 sts.

Row 2 (WS) K2, purl to last 2 sts, k2.

Beaded Floral Shawl

More than 500 silvery glass beads—applied with a crochet hook as you knit, no pre-stringing necessary—dot the center of the large and small flowers at the body and border of a shimmery silk shawl by Karen Joan Raz. Stitched top-down, it's shaped with yarn-over increases at the edges and spine.

Row 3 K2, work chart row 3, k1, work chart row 3, k2—11 sts.

Row 4 K2, purl to last 2 sts, k2. Cont to work this way through Row 24—51 sts.

Row 25 K2, *beg with first st and work across chart to beg of rep, work 12-st rep, work across to end of chart*, k1, rep from * to * once more, k2. Cont to work pat in this way through Row 36—75 sts.

Row 37 K2, *beg with first st and work across chart to beg of rep, work 12-st rep twice, work across to end of chart*, k1, rep from * to * once more, k2. Work this way through Row 48—99 sts. Cont to work the chart in this way, adding one 12-st rep to each side each time a 12-row rep has been completed, until you have worked the 12 rows a total of 14 times. Each 12 rows add 24 sts to the shawl. When Row 192 is complete, there are 387 sts total.

Set up for border

Row 193 K2, yo, k to center st, yo, k1 (center st), yo, k to last 2 sts, yo, k2—391 sts.

Row 194 K2, p to last 2 sts, k2.

Begin border

Row 195 K2, *work chart row to beg of 6-st rep, work 6-st rep 27 times, work to end of chart row*, k1; rep from * to *, k2. Cont in this way until the 6 rows of the border have been completed 6 times—463 sts. With each completed 6-row rep, one more 6-st rep is added across each side.

Set up for bind-off

Next row K2, yo, k to center st, yo, k1 (center st), yo, k to last 2 sts, yo, k2—467 sts.

Next row K2, p to last 2 sts, k2.

Bind off

Row 1 K2, yo, S2KP, turn.

Row 2 Sl 1, p1, k2, turn. Rep rows 1 and 2 until 6 sts rem. Place 3 sts on extra needle and with RS facing each other work 3 needle bind-off.

FINISHING

Block to measurements. ✛

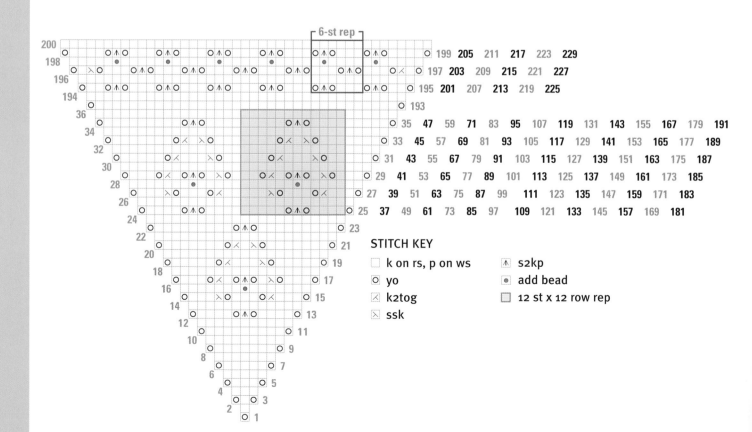

STITCH KEY

☐ k on rs, p on ws	⋀ s2kp
○ yo	• add bead
⟋ k2tog	▨ 12 st x 12 row rep
⟍ ssk	

Two-Tone Lace Shawl

This airy shawl by Meg Swansen juxtaposes tone and technique. The body, knit in a simple lace pattern, is started with a provisional cast-on that allows the pointed border to be knitted on and worked horizontally.

KNITTED MEASUREMENTS

Approx 15½"/39.5cm x 86"/218cm (measured from longest point of border)

MATERIALS

3 1¾oz/50g hanks (each approx 250yd/229m) of Schoolhouse Press *Icelandic Laceweight* (wool) in #7208 lilac (MC) (4)
1 ball in #1027 palest silver (CC)
One size 9 (5.5mm) circular needle, 24"/60cm long OR SIZE TO OBTAIN GAUGE

GAUGE

18 sts and 18 rows = 4"/10cm over lace pat using size 9 (5.5mm) needle.
TAKE TIME TO CHECK GAUGE.

PROVISIONAL CAST-ON

Leaving tails about 4"/10cm long, tie a length of scrap yarn together with the main yarn in a knot. With your right hand, hold the knot on top of the needle a short distance from the tip, then place your thumb and index finger between the two yarns and hold the long ends with the other fingers. Hold your hand with your palm facing upward and spread your thumb and index finger apart so that the yarn forms a "V" with the main yarn over your index finger and the scrap yarn over your thumb. Bring the needle up through the scrap yarn loop on your thumb from front to back. Place the needle over the main yarn on your index finger and then back through the loop on your thumb. Drop the loop off your thumb and placing your thumb back in the "V" configuration, tighten up the stitch on the needle. Repeat for the desired number of stitches. The main yarn will form the stitches on the needle and the scrap yarn will make the horizontal ridge at the base of the cast-on row.

When picking up the stitches along the cast-on edge, carefully cut and pull out the scrap yarn as you place the exposed loops on the needle. Take care to pick up the loops so that they are in the proper direction before you begin knitting.

LACE PATTERN (multiple of 9 sts plus 7)

Row 1 (RS) K3, k2tog, *yo twice, SK2P; rep from * to last 5 sts, yo twice, k2tog, k3.

Rows 2 and 4 K across and in every double yo work p1 and k1.

Row 3 K6, *k2tog, yo twice, ssk, k5; rep from *to last 6 sts, k6.

Row 5 K5, *k2tog, yo, k2, yo, ssk, k3; rep from * to last 5 sts, k5.

Rows 6 and 8 Knit.

Row 7 K4, *k2tog, yo, k4, yo, ssk, k1; rep from * to last 4 sts, k4.

Rep rows 1–8 for lace pat.

SHAWL

Using invisible cast-on, with MC cast on 70 sts. K 1 row. Work in lace pat until 8 rows of pat have been worked 37 times, then work row 1 once more.

Next row (WS) K1, [k2, k2tog] 9 times, [k3, k2tog] 6 times, k3. Leave rem 55 sts on needle.

BORDER

NOTE Border is joined to scarf sts on needle at end of every RS row.

With CC, loosely cast on 23 sts. Work in lace border as foll:

Row 1 (RS) K2, yo, [k2tog, yo] 4 times, k2, SK2P, yo twice, k2, k2tog, yo, k3, k last st tog with first st of shawl sts.

Row 2 K2, k2tog, yo, k4, p1 and k1 into double yo, k12, k2tog, yo.

Row 3 K1 tbl into yo, k1, yo, [k2tog, yo] 4 times, k2, k2tog, k4, k2tog, yo, k3, k last st tog with first st of shawl sts.

Row 4 K2, k2tog, yo, k18, k2tog, yo.

Row 5 K1 tbl into yo, k1, yo, [k2tog, yo] 4 times, k1, SK2P, yo twice, k2tog, yo twice, k2, k2tog, yo, k3, k last st tog with first st of shawl sts.

Row 6 K2, k2tog, yo, k4, [p1 and k1 into double yo, k1] twice, k10, k2tog, yo.

Row 7 K1 tbl into yo, k1, yo, [k2tog, yo] 4 times, k10, k2tog, yo, k3, k last st tog with first st of shawl sts.

Row 8 K2, k2tog, yo, k21, k2tog, yo.

Row 9 K1 tbl into yo, k1, yo, [k2tog, yo] 4 times, k1, [SK2P, yo twice] 2 times, k2tog, yo twice, k2, k2tog, yo, k3, k last st tog with first st of shawl sts.

Row 10 K2, k2tog, yo, k4, [p1 and k1 into double yo, k1] 3 times, k10, k2tog, yo.

Row 11 K1 tbl into yo, k1, yo, [k2tog, yo] 4 times, k13, k2tog, yo, k3, k last st tog with first st of shawl sts.

Row 12 K2, k2tog, yo, k24, k2tog, yo.

Row 13 K1 tbl into yo, k1, yo, [k2tog, yo] 4 times, k1, [SK2P, yo twice] 3 times, k2tog, yo twice, k2, k2tog, yo, k3, k last st tog with first st of shawl sts.

Row 14 K2, k2tog, yo, k4, [p1 and k1 into double yo, k1] 4 times, k10, k2tog, yo.

Row 15 K1 tbl into yo, k1, yo, [k2tog, yo] 4 times, k16, k2tog, yo, k3, k last st tog with first st of shawl sts.

Row 16 K2, k2tog, yo, k27, k2tog, yo—33 sts.

Row 17 Bind off 10 sts, k until there are 17 sts on RH needle, k2tog, yo, k3, k last st tog with first st of shawl sts—23 sts.

Row 18 K2, k2tog, yo, k17, k2tog, yo.

Rep rows 1–18 five time more. Bind off all sts, working last st of border tog with last st on shawl.

Carefully cut waste yarn on cast-on edge and slip sts to needle.

Next row K1, [k2, k2tog] 9 times, [k3, k2tog] 6 times, k3. Leave rem 55 sts on needle. Work border on this edge as before.

FINISHING

Block to measurements. ✛

Pinwheel Shawl

An alluring wrap shawl by Teva Durham flows and form-fits. Held in place with a button-loop closure, the turquoise piece is constructed from pinwheel medallions worked separately and sewn together.

■■■□

KNITTED MEASUREMENTS

Pinwheel (point-to-point) 13"/33cm
Cape approx 40"/101.5cm wide

MATERIALS

4 1¾oz/50g balls (each approx 163yd/147m) of Loop-d-Loop by Teva Durham/Tahki•Stacy Charles, Inc. *Moss* (extrafine merino wool/nylon) in #4 turquoise (3)
One set (4) size 9 (5.5mm) double-pointed needles OR SIZE TO OBTAIN GAUGE
One size 9 (5.5mm) circular needle, 16"/40cm length
One size I-9 (5.5mm) crochet hook
Stitch marker
One 1"/25mm button
Tapestry needle

GAUGE

16 sts and 20 rnds = 4"/10cm over St st using size 9 (5.5mm) needles.
TAKE TIME TO CHECK GAUGE.

NOTE

On even rnds, work double and triple yarnovers as 1 st, dropping extra loops.

PINWHEEL MEDALLION (make 7)

With dpn, cast on 3 sts. P 1 row on WS. Distribute sts evenly over 3 dpns, place marker and join for knitting in the round. Inc as foll, changing to circular needle when sts no longer comfortably fit on dpns.
Rnd 1 [Yo, k1] 3 times—6 sts.
Rnd 2 and all even rnds Knit.
Rnd 3 [Yo, k1] 6 times—12 sts.
Rnd 5 [Yo wrapping yarn twice around needle, k1] 12 times—24 sts.
Rnd 7 [Yo wrapping yarn twice around needle, k4] 6 times—30 sts.
Rnd 9 [Yo wrapping yarn twice around needle, k5] 6 times—36 sts.
Rnd 11 [Yo wrapping yarn 3 times around needle, k6] 6 times—42 sts.
Rnd 13 [Yo wrapping yarn 3 times around needle, k7] 6 times—48 sts.
Rnd 15 [Yo wrapping yarn 3 times around needle, k8] 6 times—54 sts.
Rnd 17 *Yo wrapping yarn 3 times around needle, k1, yo wrapping yarn 3 times around needle, ssk, k6; rep from * around—60 sts.
Rnd 19 *Yo wrapping yarn 3 times around needle, k3, yo wrapping yarn 3 times around needle, ssk, k5; rep from * around—66 sts.
Rnd 21 *Yo wrapping yarn 3 times around needle, k5, yo wrapping yarn 3 times around needle, ssk, k4; rep from * around—72 sts.
Rnd 23 *Yo wrapping yarn 3 times around needle, k7, yo wrapping yarn 3 times around needle, ssk, k3; rep from * around—78 sts.
Rnd 25 *Yo wrapping yarn 3 times around needle, k9, yo wrapping yarn 3 times around

needle, ssk, k2; rep from * around—84 sts.

Rnd 27 *Yo wrapping yarn 3 times around needle, k11, yo wrapping yarn 3 times around needle, ssk, k1; rep from * around—90 sts. Bind off loosely.

FINISHING

Block each pinwheel to measurements. Arrange using diagram for reference and sl st crochet in place (see photos below). Follow diagram and sl st the two "A" sides tog, then sl st the two "B" sides tog. Sew button to left side of front neck opening.

Button loop

With crochet hook, chain a loop on the right side of neck, wide enough to allow button to pass through. Secure to opposite button. ⊹

**MEDALLION
PLACEMENT
DIAGRAM**

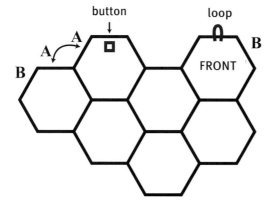

JOINING MEDALLIONS WITH SLIPSTITCH

1. Place the wrong sides of two medallions together on a flat surface. Insert a crochet hook under the bound-off edge on both pieces, as shown.

2. Draw the yarn through the knitting and through the loop on the hook to complete the slipstitch.

Starfish Shawl

In Kristin Omdahl's lacy shawl, netted starfish are made separately as six-sided motifs, assembled into a half-circle shape and finished off with a knitted-on border. Subtly dyed yarn creates depth and calls to mind the deep blue shades of the ocean.

■■■□

KNITTED MEASUREMENTS
Motif (point to point) 14"/35.5cm
Shawl 62" x 40"/157.5cm x 101.5cm

MATERIALS
2 6oz/170g skeins (each approx 675yd/617m) of
The Great Adirondack Yarn Company *Sireno*
(silk/merino wool) in bella blue (4)
One set (4) size 5 (3.75mm) dpn OR SIZE TO
OBTAIN GAUGE
One size 5 (3.75mm) circular needle, 16"/40cm
length
Stitch marker
Tapestry needle

GAUGES
1 motif = 14"/35.5cm after blocking.

14 sts and 18 rnds = 4"/10cm in blocked flower
motif.
TAKE TIME TO CHECK GAUGES.

STITCH GLOSSARY
Double Inc
[K1, yo, k1] into next st—3 sts.

MOTIF (make 9)
Make slip knot and place on dpn. With second
needle, [k1, p1] 6 times into slip knot—12 sts.
Distribute sts evenly over 3 needles, place
marker and join for knitting in the round.
Rnd 1 Knit.
Rnd 2 *Yo, k1; rep from * to marker—24 sts.
Rnd 3 Knit.
Beg chart
Rep chart 6 times around. Work through rnd 29,

changing to circular needle when sts no longer comfortably fit on dpns. Bind off as foll: K1, *yo, k1, sl first k st and yo up and over last st and off needles; rep from * around.

FINISHING

Block motifs. Sew motifs together, using diagram as guide.

Ruffle edging

Cast on 10 sts.

Foundation row Knit.

Row 1 (RS) K9, sl last st, with RS of shawl facing, pick up and knit stitch on edge of shawl, pass sl st over.

Row 2 Knit.

Rows 3–6 Rep rows 1 and 2.

Row 7 [Yo, k2tog] 4 times, turn.

Row 8 K8.

Row 9 [Yo, k2tog] 3 times, turn.

Row 10 K6.

Row 11 [Yo, k2tog] twice, turn.

Row 12 Knit 4. Rep rows 1–12 around entire edge of shawl.

Graft last row of edging to cast-on edge.

Block shawl to measurements. ✢

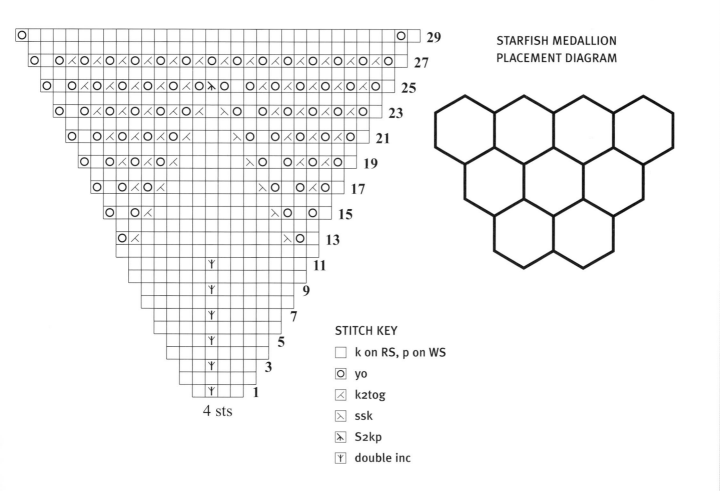

STARFISH MEDALLION PLACEMENT DIAGRAM

4 sts

STITCH KEY

☐ k on RS, p on WS

⊙ yo

╱ k2tog

╲ ssk

⅄ S2kp

⅄ double inc

Wrapped

Bold and beautiful shawls
set the stage for striking
stripes, lovely Fair Isle, and
eye-catching color blocks.

in Color

■□□□

KNITTED MEASUREMENTS

Approx 27" x 84"/68.5cm x 213cm with edging

MATERIALS

Various 4-ply yarns and colors from Rowan/
Westminster Fibers, Inc.
One pair size 3 (3.25mm) needles OR SIZE TO
OBTAIN GAUGE
Size D/3 (3.25mm) crochet hook

GAUGE

28 sts and 40 rows = 4"/10cm over St st using
size 3 (3.25mm) needles.
TAKE TIME TO CHECK GAUGE.

WRAP

Cast on 180 sts with desired color. Work in St st,
working first and last st in garter st for selvage
sts, using colors and yarns as desired, for
83"/211cm, or desired length. Bind off.

EDGING

With RS facing, crochet hook and desired color,
work evenly around entire outside edge as foll:
Next rnd *Sc, ch 1, skip 1 st (or row); rep from *
evenly around outside edge, working (sc, ch 1,
sc, ch 1) in each corner.
Next 3 rnds With desired color work sc, ch 1 in
each ch-1 sp. Fasten off.

FINISHING

Weave in ends. Block to measurements. ✛

Striped Wrap

Several years ago, while teaching color
workshops, Brandon Mably, of the Kaffe
Fassett Studio, started collecting leftover
bits of yarn; during class and in his
downtime, he began knitting them
together. Colors were chosen randomly—
then, if sections became too dark, a
kickier color was added; too acidic, a
somber hue was introduced to tone it
down. What evolved is this glorious wrap.
You can easily vary the length to create a
more slender scarf or a beautiful blanket.

■■■■

KNITTED MEASUREMENTS

At widest point 27"/68.5cm, including border

Length from top center back to lower edge

9"/23cm

MATERIALS

Original Yarn

2 1¾oz/50g balls (each approx 153yd/140m) of
Lana Gatto *Feeling* (wool/silk/cashmere) in
#10009 cream (MC) **3**

1 ball each in #13340 loden (A), #12942 olive
green (B), #12732 moss (C), #12246 cranberry
(D), #12947 vieux rose (E), #10107 burgundy (F),
#12940 plum (G)

Substitute Yarn

3 1¾oz/50g skeins (each approx 137yd/125m) of
Debbie Bliss/KFI *Baby Cashmerino* (merino wool/
microfiber/cashmere) in #101 off white (MC) **3**

1 ball each in #8 midnight blue (A), #503 pea
green (B), #24 hunter (C), #34 cherry (D), #13
grape (E), #28 wine (F), #608 light lilac (G)

One pair each sizes 5 and 6 (3.75 and 4mm)
needles

Yarn needle (optional for duplicate stitch)

GAUGE

23 sts and 28 rows to 4"/10cm over St st using
larger needles.

TAKE TIME TO CHECK GAUGE.

NOTES

1) Floral design is knitted-in. For an alternate
method, knit capelet chart in cream only and
then work design in duplicate st after.

2) One-half of chart is shown. Work each row of
chart to center and then back to beg.

Floral Capelet

Alison Dupernex's flower-strewn capelet
looks ever-so-sexy slipped over bare
shoulders or a tiny tee. It's knit in one
piece; the borders and ties are worked
separately and sewn on.

CAPELET

With MC and larger needles, cast on 66 sts
and p 1 row on WS. Work in St st and beg with
row 1 (RS) of chart, inc sts to shape capelet
as specified. To add more than 1 st at beg and
end of row, cast on sts. On row 59 of chart,
work to center 48 sts, join a 2nd ball of yarn
and bind off center 48 sts, work to end.
Working each side separately, complete left
and right sides of chart.

BORDER AND TIES

Outside border/ties

With smaller needles and MC, cast on 6 sts. Work
in rib for 94"/40cm. Bind off.

Inside border

Work as for outside border to a length of
30"/78cm.

FINISHING

If desired, work duplicate st for floral chart.
Block capelet. Mark the center point of the
longer piece of ribbing and position it at the
center back on outside edge of capelet. Fit and
pin border to outside edge of capelet and
sew in place. (The excess at each end is for the
ties.) Sew shorter border piece to back neck
edge of capelet. ✣

COLOR KEY

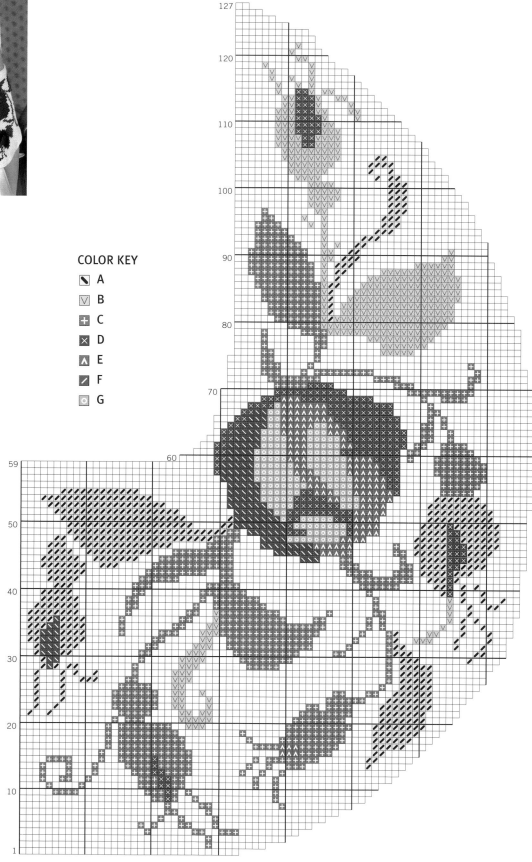

- A
- B
- C
- D
- E
- F
- G

Squares Shawl

Kaffe Fassett, known for his ingenious color combinations, uses simple shapes to showcase his artistic flair. This strikingly multicolored intarsia shawl can be made longer by repeating the squares or narrower by working half the chart. Various rectangular motifs sandwich the main patterning at either end.

■■□□

KNITTED MEASUREMENTS

Approx 16" x 60"/40.5cm x 152.5cm

MATERIALS

1 .88oz/25g ball (each approx 120yd/110m) Rowan/Westminster Fibers, Inc. *Scottish Tweed 4-Ply* (wool) in #4 storm grey (B), #13 claret (C), #18 thatch (D), #23 midnight (E), #14 heath (F), #6 sea green (G), #16 thistle (H), #15 apple (I), #3 skye (J) #17 lobster (K), #9 rust (L), #19 peat (M), #2 machair (N), #5 lavender (o), #7 lewis grey (P), #11 sunset (Q), #22 celtic mix (R), #1 grey mist (S), #20 mallard (T), #12 wine (U) (**NOTE** There is no color A used in this pattern.) **2**
One pair size 4 (3.5)mm needles OR SIZE TO OBTAIN GAUGE

GAUGE

22 sts and 34 rows = 4"/10cm over St st using size 4 (3.5mm) needles.
TAKE TIME TO CHECK GAUGE.

SHAWL

With E and size 4 (3.5mm) needles, cast on 90 sts. Work 2 rows in garter st. Change to St st for 3 more rows, keeping first and last 2 sts of each row in garter st.

Beg chart

Cont to work in St st with first and last 2 sts of each row in garter st, foll chart. When chart is complete, with E work 3 rows in St st, keeping first and last 2 sts in St st. Work next 2 rows in garter st. Bind off. ✤

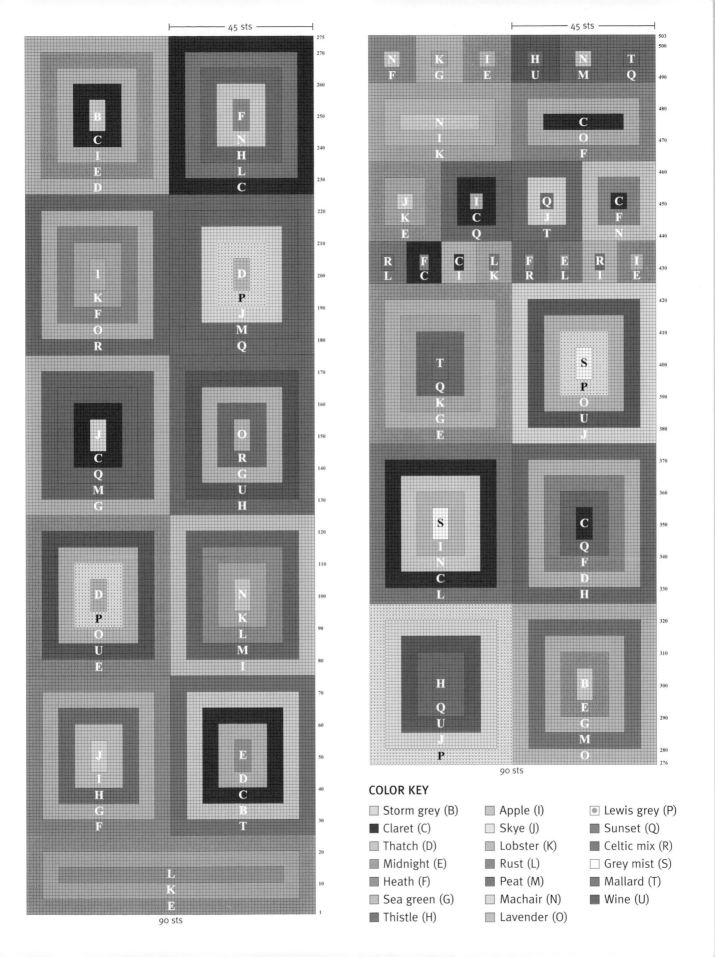

COLOR KEY

- ☐ Storm grey (B)
- ■ Claret (C)
- ☐ Thatch (D)
- ■ Midnight (E)
- ■ Heath (F)
- ☐ Sea green (G)
- ■ Thistle (H)

- ☐ Apple (I)
- ☐ Skye (J)
- ☐ Lobster (K)
- ■ Rust (L)
- ■ Peat (M)
- ☐ Machair (N)
- ☐ Lavender (O)

- ☉ Lewis grey (P)
- ■ Sunset (Q)
- ■ Celtic mix (R)
- ☐ Grey mist (S)
- ■ Mallard (T)
- ■ Wine (U)

Cashmere Rainbow Shawl

Linda Morse's colorful shawl is knit from the top down in an easy increase pattern.

■■□□

KNITTED MEASUREMENTS
Neck 16"/40.5cm
Length approx 35"/89cm

MATERIALS

Original Yarn
1 1¾oz/50g ball (approx 126yd/115m) of S. Charles Collezione/Tahki•Stacy Charles, Inc. *Cashmere Breeze* (cashmere) in #303566 pink (B) and #303326 dark pink (C) ④
2 balls each in #303324 dark blue (A), #303331 red (D), #303329 orange (E), #303328 light orange (F), #303327 yellow (G), #303337 lime (H), #303321 light blue (I), #303323 blue (J)

Substitute Yarn
1 1¾oz/50g ball (each approx 137yd/125m) of Filatura Di Crosa/Tahki•Stacy Charles, Inc. *Zara* (merino wool) in #1756 hot pink (B) and #21 bright pink (C) ③
2 balls each in #1755 violet (A), #1466 red (D), #1762 bright orange (E), #1738 melon (F), #1787 sunshine (G), #1727 kelly green (H), #1462 light blue (I) and #1737 light violet (J)
One each size 7 (4.5mm) circular needle, 32"/80cm and 47"/120cm lengths OR SIZE TO OBTAIN GAUGE
Stitch markers

GAUGE
18 sts and 29 rows to 4"/10cm over St st.
TAKE TIME TO CHECK GAUGE.

PATTERN STITCH
Row 1 (RS) [K1, M1, k to 1 st before marker, M1, k1, sl marker] 3 times, k1, M1, k to last st, M1, k1.
Row 2 (WS) Purl.
Rep rows 1 & 2 for pattern stitch.

SHAWL
With A and 32"/80cm needle, cast on 72 sts.
Next row (RS) [K18, place marker] 3 times, k to end.
Work 9 more rows even in St st.
Next row (RS) Change to B and work row 1 of pattern stitch. Changing to longer circular needle when required to accommodate number of sts, work evenly in pattern stitch for 27 more rows.
Change to C and work even in pattern stitch for 26 rows.
Change to D and work even in pattern stitch for 24 rows.
Change to E and work even in pattern stitch for 22 rows.
Change to F and work even in pattern stitch for 20 rows or to end of second ball, ending at end of row.
Change to G and work even in pattern stitch to end of second ball, ending at end of row.
Change to H and work even in pattern stitch to end of second ball, ending at end of row.
Change to I and work even in pattern stitch to end of second ball, ending at end of row.
Change to J and work even in pattern stitch to end of second ball, ending with a WS row.
Change to A and work even in pattern stitch for 6 rows.
Continuing in A, work as foll:
Row 1 (RS) [K1, k2tog, k to 3 sts before marker, ssk, k1, sl marker] 3 times, k1, k2tog, k to last 3 sts, ssk, k1.
Row 2 Purl.
Rep last 2 rows once more. Bind off.

FINISHING

Front edges
With 47"/120cm needle and A, beg at bound-off edge, work along right front and with RS facing, pick up 3 sts for every 4 rows. Work in St st for 8 rows. Bind off.
With 47"/120cm needle and A, beg at cast-on edge, work along left front and with RS facing, pick up 3 sts for every 4 rows. Work in St st for 8 rows. Bind off.
Fold front edges in half to WS. Fold cast-on and bound edges in half to WS, so that half of A becomes a hem. Sew hems to front edges, neatly mitering the corners. ✤

Geometric Wrap

■■■□

KNITTED MEASUREMENTS

Bust 72"/182.5cm

Length from shoulder 32"/81.5cm (back) and

34"/86.5cm (fronts)

MATERIALS

Original Yarn

2 3½oz/100g balls (each approx 154yd/140m) of Rowan/Westminster Fibers, Inc. *Chunky Chenille* (cotton) each in #367 black (A), #381 mauve (B), #378 med blue (C), #362 forest green (D), #387 navy (E), #356 purple (F), #382 burgundy (G), #380 rust (H), #379 brown (I), #363 olive green (J) **5**

Substitute Yarn

4 3½oz/100g skeins (each approx 98yd/90m) of Crystal Palace Yarns *Cotton Chenille* (combed cotton) in #9598 jet black (A), #1404 dark lilac (B), #8095 french blue (C), #6320 aloe (D), #9717 navy (E), #9660 purple (F), #4021 red velvet (G), #2230 mango (H), #516 cocoa (I), #4043 cypress (J) **4**

One pair size 8 (5mm) needles OR SIZE TO OBTAIN GAUGE

Size 8 (5mm) circular needle 36"/90cm long

GAUGE

16 sts and 24 rows = 4"/10cm over St st using size 8 (5mm) needles.

TAKE TIME TO CHECK GAUGE.

BACK

With A, cast on 144 sts. K 4 rows. Change to B and k 2 rows. Work in St st foll chart through row 186. This is end of back.

Kaffe Fassett goes graphic with this captivating ruana, inspired by the traditional-style wrap of South America. The "Palio" design is knit in one piece in an intarsia zigzag pattern and trimmed with garter-stitch edges.

RIGHT FRONT

Row 187 (RS) Cont chart over first 72 sts for right front, place rem 72 sts on a holder for left front. Cont in right front sts only and cont chart pat through row 383. Change to B and p 2 rows. Change to A and p 3 rows. Bind off.

LEFT FRONT

Rejoin yarn to sts on holder and complete as for right front, foll last 72 sts of chart.

FINISHING

Block to measurements.

Front edging

With circular needle and B, pick up and k 136 sts evenly along inside edge of right front and 136 sts along inside edge of left front. K 1 row. Change to A and k 2 rows. Bind off. ⊹

186
180
170
160
150
140
130
120
110
100
90
80
70
60
50
40
30
20
10
1

144 sts

COLOR KEY

- A
- B
- C
- D
- B
- F
- G
- H
- I
- J

383
380

370

360

350

340

330

320

310

300

290

280

270

260

250

240

230

220

210

200

190
187

Fold line

Wave Pattern Wrap

Rebecca Rosen's medley of texture springs from a drop-stitch pattern that delivers fast and fabulous results. The drama comes from a mélange of gorgeous hand-dyed yarns.

■■□□

KNITTED MEASUREMENTS

Approx 25" x 80"/63.5cm x 203cm

MATERIALS

1 3½oz/100g hank (each approx 55yd/50m) of Colinette Yarns/Unique Kolours, Ltd. *Point 5* (wool) each in undyed and #144 cream tea (6)

1 3½oz/100g hank (each approx 191yd/175m) of Colinette Yarns/Unique Kolours, Ltd. *Mohair* (mohair/wool/nylon) each in #63 mushroom, undyed and #144 cream tea (4)

1 3½oz/100g hank (approx 110yd/100m) of Colinette Yarns/Unique Kolours, Ltd. *Fandango* (cotton) in undyed (6)

1 3½oz/100g hank (approx 186yd/170m) of Colinette Yarns/Unique Kolours, Ltd. *Wigwam* (cotton) in #144 cream tea (4)

1 3½oz/100g hank (approx 110yd/100m) of Colinette Yarns/Unique Kolours, Ltd. *Isis* (viscose) in #144 cream tea (6)

1 3½oz/100g hank (each approx 103yd/94m) of Colinette Yarns/Unique Kolours, Ltd. *Zanziba* (wool/viscose/nylon) each in #63 mushroom and undyed (4)

One pair size 19 (15mm) needles OR SIZE TO OBTAIN GAUGE

GAUGE

9 sts = 4"/10cm over wave pat using size 19 (15mm) needles.
TAKE TIME TO CHECK GAUGE.

WAVE PATTERN

(multiple of 10 sts plus 6)

Rows 1 and 2 Knit.

Row 3 K6, *(yo) once, k1, (yo) twice, k1, (yo) 3 times, k1, (yo) twice, k1, (yo) once, k6; rep from * to end.

Row 4 K, dropping all yos.

Rows 5 and 6 Knit.

Row 7 K1; rep from * of row 3, end k1 instead of k6.

Row 8 Rep row 4.

Rep rows 1–8 for wave pat.

WRAP

Cast on 56 sts with desired color. Work in wave pat, using colors and yarns as desired, for 80"/203cm, or desired length. Bind off.

FINISHING

Weave in ends. Block to measurements. ✤

■■■◻

KNITTED MEASUREMENTS

18"/45.5cm wide by 54"/137cm long (length is measured from inside joining point of back neck)

MATERIALS

Original Yarn

6 1¾oz/50g skeins (each approx 148yd/136m) of Dale of Norway *Sisik* (wool/mohair/acrylic/viscose) in #160 olive tweed (MC) (3)
2 1¾oz/50g balls (each approx 126yd/116m) of Dale of Norway *Tiur* (mohair/wool) each in #9853 olive (A), #2343 khaki (B) and #9835 lt olive (C) (3)

Substitute Yarn

8 1¾oz/50g balls (each approx 120yd/110m) of Classic Elite Yarns *Portland Tweed* (virgin wool/alpaca/viscose) in #5015 flourite green (MC) (4)
3 1½oz/42g (each approx 90yd/82m) of Classic Elite Yarns *La Gran* (mohair/wool/nylon) each in #6539 eucalyptus green (A), #6575 pebble (B) and #6572 underappreciated green (C) (4)
One pair size 5 (3.75mm) needles OR SIZE TO OBTAIN GAUGE
Size 5 (3.75mm) circular needle, 29"/74cm long

GAUGE

18 sts and 25 rows = 4"/10cm over pat st (after blocking) using size 5 (3.75mm) needles.
TAKE TIME TO CHECK GAUGE.

NOTE

When changing colors in pat st, carry MC along sides of rows. Cut colors A, B and C and rejoin at each color stripe.

Zigzag Stole

Barbara Venishnick's seasonless lightweight wrap is a clever construction of two rectangles, one long, one short. Worked in a textured mosaic pattern, the pieces are sewn at right angles to form a V.

LONG RECTANGLE

With straight needles and MC, cast on 81 sts. Work the next 3 preparation rows as foll:
Preparation row 1 (WS) Purl.
Preparation row 2 (RS) Knit.
Preparation row 3 (WS) P2, *wrapping yarn around needle twice, p1, then p3; rep from * ending last rep p2 instead of p3.

Beg pat st

Row 1 (RS) With A, k2, *sl 1 st wyib, then dropping the extra wrap, k1 st, insert RH needle into the next st 2 rows below and pull up a loop loosely, k the next st, pass the loop over the st just knit, k1; rep from *, end sl 1 wyib, k2.
Row 2 With A, p2, *sl 1 wyif, p3; rep from *, end sl 1 wyif, p2.
Row 3 With A, knit.
Row 4 With A, p2, * wrapping yarn twice around needle, p1, p 3; rep from *, end last rep p2 instead of p3.
Rows 5–8 With MC, rep rows 1–4.
Rows 9–12 With B, rep rows 1–4.
Rows 13–16 With MC, rep rows 1–4.
Rows 17–20 With C, rep rows 1–4.
Rows 21–24 With MC, rep rows 1–4.
Rep these 24 rows for pat st until piece measures approx 54"/137cm from beg, ending with row 3 in MC.

Short edge trim

Next row (WS) With MC, *k3, k2tog, k4; rep from * 8 times more—72 sts.

Next row (RS) Purl.

Next row (WS) Knit. Bind off all sts purlwise.

Lengthwise trim

With RS facing, circular needle and MC, working along the left edge of the piece, pick up and k 1 st in every other row along side edge of piece to the trim, leave side of trim free. K1 row, p1 row, k1 row. Bind off all sts purlwise.

SHORT RECTANGLE

Work as for long rectangle until piece measures 36"/92cm. Work short-edge trim and left-side lengthwise trim as for long rectangle. Pin the cast-on edge of the short rectangle to the right side of the long rectangle underneath the trim (see diagram) stretching slightly. Sew this edge in place.

Final lengthwise trim

With RS facing, circular needle and MC, pick up and k 72 sts along the cast-on edge of the long rectangle then cont along the side edge of the short rectangle, picking up 1 st in every other row to lower edge. Work trim as for previous trims.

FINISHING

Block flat to measurements. Sew ends of trims tog at corners. ✢

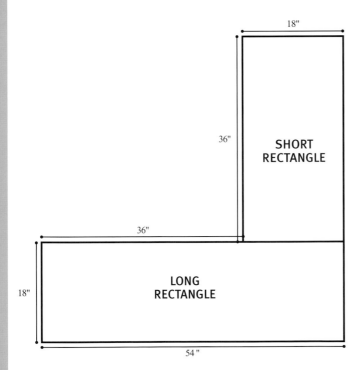

Patchwork Wrap

Valentina Devine takes a geometric approach in this colorful shawl. Diagonal garter-stitch squares are knit separately in two hues, then sewn or crocheted together. The yarn ends are crocheted on the right side in a free-form organic pattern.

■■■▯

KNITTED MEASUREMENTS

Approx 24" x 72"/61cm x 183cm (not including fringe)

MATERIALS

2 2oz/57g skeins (each approx 118yd/108m) of La Lana Wools *Forever Random Fine* (wool) each in moonmist (A), emerald city (B), monet (C), yellow brick road (D), sweet lorraine (E), apassionada (F) and noche (G) (**5**)

1 skein each in deep sea indigo glace (H), fairy queen (I), zulu prince (J) and rosemist (K)

One pair size 10½ (6.5mm) needles OR SIZE TO OBTAIN GAUGE

Size H/8 (5mm) crochet hook

GAUGES

14 sts and 32 rows = 4"/10 cm over garter st using size 10½ (6.5mm) needles.

One square = 6"/15cm using size 10½ (6.5mm) needles.

TAKE TIME TO CHECK GAUGES.

NOTE

To change color when working in sc, draw new color through 2 lps on hook to complete sc.

SQUARE (make 48)

Refer to color placement diagram. With color 1, cast on 2 sts.

Next row Knit. Cont in garter st, inc 1 st at beg of next 28 rows—30 sts. Cut yarn, leaving a 25"/63.5cm tail. Join color 2 with a knot leaving a 25"/63.5cm tail (tails are used for crochet

embellishments). Cont in garter st, dec 1 st at beg of next 28 rows—2 sts. Cut yarn, draw through sts.

Embellishments

Crochet embellishments are worked freeform. You can create zigzag, straight or curved lines as foll: Position square so tails are at RH side. From RS with hook and color 1 tail, make a slip knot at base of tail and place on hook. Working on color 2 side, ch 3, sl st in a st, *ch 3, sl st in desired st; rep from * until a 3"/7.5cm tail rem, or you have completed desired design. Fasten off. Using color 2 tail, embellish color 1 side.

FINISHING

Sew squares tog foll placement diagram so that embellishments are at top left corner.

Edging

With RS facing and hook, join C with a sl st in top right corner. Making sure that work lies flat, sc evenly around entire edge, changing colors to match colors of squares and working 3 sc in each corner. Join rnd with a sl st in first sc. Ch 1, turn to WS.

Fringe row *Ch 40, sl st in next st, sc in next st; rep from * across right side edge, bottom edge and left side edge, changing colors to match colors of squares. Ch 1, turn to RS.

Top edge Working from left to right, sc in each st across, changing colors to match colors of squares. Fasten off. ✢

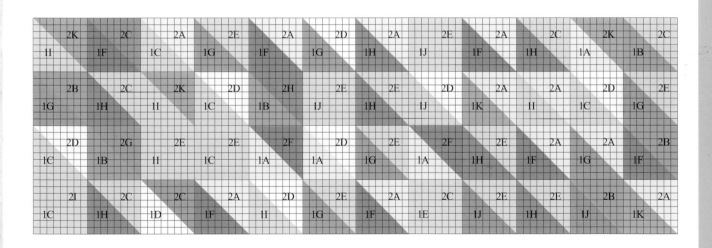

COLOR KEY

- ☐ Moonmist (A)
- ☐ Emerald city (B)
- ☐ Monet (C)
- ☐ Yellow brick road (D)
- ☐ Sweet lorraine (E)
- ☐ Apassionada (F)
- ☐ Noche (G)
- ☐ Deep sea indigo glace (H)
- ☐ Fairy queen (I)
- ☐ Zulu prince (J)
- ☐ Rosemist (K)

KNITTED MEASUREMENTS

(including band trim)

Width at top edge 35"/89cm

Depth at center 19"/48cm

MATERIALS

1 1¾oz/50g hank (each approx 110yd/100m) of Blue Sky Alpacas *Sport Weight* (baby alpaca) each in #533 navy blue (A), #511 red (B), #521 tangerine (C), #537 buttercup (D), #505 natural taupe (E), #516 petal pink (F), #510 black (G), #535 bluejay (H), #527 chartreuse (I) and #520 avocado (J) 🔲

One pair size 5 (3.75mm) needles OR SIZE TO OBTAIN GAUGE

Size 5 (3.75mm) circular needle, 24"/60cm long

One 1⅛-inch/30mm decorative button

GAUGE

26 sts and 29 rows = 4"/10cm over St st and chart pat using size 5 (3.75mm) needles.

TAKE TIME TO CHECK GAUGE.

NOTES

1) When working chart pat, carry yarn loosely at back of work to prevent puckering of fabric when changing colors.

2) Use straight needles until there are too many sts to fit comfortably on needle, then change to circular needle.

3) Chart represents center 58 sts only, cont to center pat bands while increasing foll instructions.

SHORT ROW WRAPPING

(wrap and turn—w&t)

Knit side

1) Wyib, sl next st purlwise.

Turkish Cape

Vibrant bands of Turkish-inspired motifs define this design by Mari Lynn Patrick, the curves of which are gently shaped with short rows. Worked in baby alpaca yarn, it buttons at the front.

2) Move yarn between the needles to the front.

3) Sl the same st back to LH needle. Turn work, bring yarn to the p side between needles. One st is wrapped. When short rows are completed, work to just before wrapped st, insert RH needle under the wrap and knitwise into the wrapped st, k them tog.

Purl side

1) Wyif, sl next st purlwise.

2) Move yarn between the needles to the back of work.

3) Sl same st back to LH needle. Turn work, bring yarn back to the p side between the needles. One st is wrapped. When short rows are completed, work to just before wrapped st, insert RH needle from behind into the back lp of the wrap and place on LH needle; P wrap tog with st on needle.

CAPE

Beg at lower edge with B, cast on 58 sts. Beg with row 1 of chart, cont to foll chart with shaping AT SAME TIME as foll: work 1 row of chart, then cast on 4 sts at beg of next 18 rows, 2 sts at beg of next 38 rows, 1 st at beg of next 30 rows—236 sts. Cont to foll chart, working even without shaping, through row 95.

Top shaping

Row 96 With G, p62, [p2tog] 56 times, p62.

Beg short rows

Cont to foll chart, working rem short rows each side in 3rd color band (colors F, J & E) as foll:

Next row (RS) Work 62 sts, wrap & turn (w&t).

Next row Purl to end.

Next (short) row (RS) Work 49 sts, w&t.

Next row Purl to end.

Next (short) row (RS) Work 36 sts, w&t.

Next row Purl to end.

Next (short) row (RS) Work 26 sts, w&t, work 2 sts, bind off 4 sts using 1-row buttonhole method, work until there are 26 sts on RH needle, w&t.

Next row Purl to end.

Next row (RS) K62, closing up holes. Cut yarn. Rejoin J to work the last 62 sts in short-row shaping and work shaping in reverse through end of chart. All sts on needle are now in (black) G and next row should be a WS or purl row.

Work band pattern

Beg with row 2 of band pat chart, work band pat on the 180 sts, AT SAME TIME, inc 1 st each end of every row through row 14.

Next row (RS) With G, purl (for turning ridge). With single color as desired, work 13 rows in St st (for facing) AT SAME TIME, dec 1 st each end of every row. Bind off.

FINISHING

Block to measurements.

Lower edge

To work around the shaped lower edge of cape, with G, pick up and k 282 sts evenly around the entire shaped edge of cape. Work band pat foll chart as for top edge. Fold edges to WS and sew in place. Sew on button.

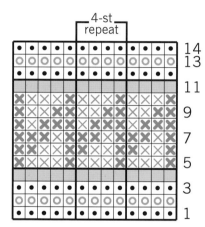

Band Pattern

COLOR KEY

☒	Tangerine (C)	⊙	Natural taupe (E)
▨	Buttercup (D)	•	Black (G)
☒	Avocado (J)		

Row 1

58 sts

COLOR KEY

- ■ Navy blue (A)
- ☒ Red (B)
- ☒ Tangerine (C)
- ▦ Buttercup (D)
- ◎ Natural taupe (E)
- ▫ Petal pink (F)
- • Black (G)
- ◉ Bluejay (H)
- ▣ Chartreuse (I)
- ☒ Avocado (J)

Warm

Chase away the chill
in these soft, luxurious
knits. Cozy never
looked so stylish!

&Cozy

■■■▢

SIZES

S/M (L/XL)

KNITTED MEASUREMENTS

Width 14 (15½)"/35.5 (39.5)cm

Length, not including 2"/5cm fringe at each end of wrap, 42½ (46)"/108 (117)cm

MATERIALS

6 (8) 3½oz/100g skeins (each approx 131yd/120m of Naturally NZ/Fiber Trends *Naturelle 14-Ply* (wool) in #552 brown tweed ⑤

One size 10 (6mm) circular, 24"/60cm long needle OR SIZE TO OBTAIN GAUGE

Two size 10 (6mm) dpn for knitted fringe

Cable needle and tapestry needle

GAUGE

23 sts and 21 rows = 4"/10cm over pat st using size 10 (6mm) needles. See note below for test swatch.

TAKE TIME TO CHECK GAUGE.

NOTES

1) To make test swatch, cast on 24 sts and work rows 1–14 of pat st once, then rows 1-8 once.

2) Fringe is worked at one end before binding off and at opposite end by picking up and working along the cast-on edge.

STITCH GLOSSARY

8-st RC Sl next 4 sts to cn and hold in *back*, k4, k4 from cn.

8-st LC Sl next 4 sts to cn and hold in *front*, k4, k4 from cn.

Cable Wrap

Teva Durham's warm, wonderful shawl uses a bulky yarn and an easy braid pattern that speeds stitching along and boosts insulation. I-cord loops create the decorative fringed ends.

PATTERN STITCH

Foundation row (WS) Purl.

Row 1 (RS) *Work 8-st RC; rep from * to end.

Rows 2–6 Work in St st, starting with a p row.

Row 7 (RS) K4, *8-st LC; rep from * to last 4 sts, k4.

Rows 8–14 Work in St st, starting with a p row.

Rep rows 1–14 for pat st.

WRAP

With circular needle, cast on 80 (88) sts.

Rep rows 1–14 of pat st 16 (18) times, then work rows 1 and 2 once more. Do not bind off.

FINISHING

Loop fringe

With dpn, *k4, turn and cont in St st on 4 sts until piece measures 4"/10cm from beg. Bind off, leaving a yarn end for sewing. With RS facing, join yarn in next st on LH needle; rep from * until all sts have been worked as loop fringe and bound off.

With dpn and RS of cast-on end of scarf facing, pick up and k 1 st in each of first 4 sts; work fringe in same way as for bound-off end of scarf until all sts have been worked.

Fold each fringe end to WS and sew bound-off edge to foundation row to form a loop. ✣

■□□□

KNITTED MEASUREMENTS

Approx 54" x 22"/137cm x 56cm (folded)

MATERIALS

Original Yarn

15 1¾oz/50g balls (each approx 65yd/60m) of Trendsetter Yarns *Liberty* (wool/nylon/acrylic) in #123 green multi (A) (5)

2 1¾oz/50g balls (each approx 95yd/87m) of Trendsetter Yarns *Sunshine* (viscose/polyester) in #48 olive (B) (4)

1 3½oz/100g ball (approx 120yd/110m) of Trendsetter Yarns *Segue* (nylon) in #123 sage (C) (6)

Substitute Yarn

7 3½oz/100g balls (each approx 155yd/142m) of Trendsetter Yarns *Treasure* (wool/acrylic/nylon) in #2102 aqua baroque (A) (4)

2 1¾oz/50g balls (each approx 95yd/87m) of Trendsetter Yarns *Sunshine* (viscose/polyester) in #48 olive (B) (4) (same as original yarn)

1 3½oz/100g ball (approx 120yd/110m) of Trendsetter Yarns *Segue* (nylon) in #123 sage (6) (same as original yarn)

One pair size 11 (8mm) needles OR SIZE TO OBTAIN GAUGE

Size I/9 (5.5mm) crochet hook

Stitch markers

Six 2"/50mm buttons

GAUGE

16 sts and 20 rows = 4"/10cm over St st using *Liberty* or *Treasure* yarn (A) and size 11 (8mm) needles.

TAKE TIME TO CHECK GAUGE.

Oversized Wrap

Stitched in an oversized rectangle, Fayla Reiss's reversible design does double duty as a shrug or coat. The trim is crocheted, and buttons create sleeves or a vent.

WRAP

With A, cast on 215 sts. Work in St st until piece measures 14"/35.5cm. Pm each end. Cont in St st until piece measures 33"/84cm from beg. Bind off.

FINISHING

Place piece flat. Attach buttons on marked row, beg 1"/2.5cm in from each end then working 2"/5cm apart for a total of 3 buttons each end.

Crochet edging

With RS facing, crochet hook and C, work 1 row sc evenly around outside edge of piece, making button loops opposite buttons as foll: ch 14, join with sl st to first ch. Do not turn. Work backwards sc (from left to right) in each sc, working in front loop of each st. Change to 2 strands B and work 1 row reverse sc in the back half of each sc to create a 2nd layer of roped edge.

Fold piece over and secure loops over buttons. Slip arms through opening for sleeves and wear as a shrug jacket. Or, secure loops over buttons. Turn piece upside down. Place arms into sleeves and allow wrap to roll up and around body. ✤

■■■◻

SIZES

S/L (XL/2X)

KNITTED MEASUREMENTS

Bust (closed) 53½ (61½)"/136 (156)cm

Length 30½ (33½)"/77.5 (85)cm

MATERIALS

8 (10) 3½oz/100g balls (each approx 45yd/41m)
of Gedifra/Westminster Fibers, Inc. *Highland
Alpaca* (alpaca/wool) in #2905 lilac **6**

Size 19 (15mm) circular needle 60"/150cm long
OR SIZE TO OBTAIN GAUGE

One set (4) size 19 (15mm) dpn

GAUGE

8 sts and 10 rows = 4"/10cm over trinity st using
size 19 (15mm) needle.

TAKE TIME TO CHECK GAUGE.

NOTE

Due to the oversized silhouette of this garment,
it will fit a large range of sizes.

TRINITY STITCH

(over a multiple of 4 sts plus 3)

Row 1 (WS) K2, *p3tog, k in front, back and front
of next st; rep from * to last 2 sts, end k2.

Rows 2 and 4 Purl.

Row 3 K2, *k in front, back and front of next st (to
make 3 sts in 1), p3tog; rep from *, to last 2 sts,
end k2.

NOTE At the end of every pat row 1, there will be
2 less sts in the row. Then at the end of every pat
row 3, there will be 2 more sts and back to the
original number) Rep rows 1–4 for trinity st.

Textured Cape
Faith Hale's dolman cover-up is knit in
one piece from the deep ribbed bottom
edge up through the trinity-stitch body.
The front and collar bands are picked up
and worked in seed stitch, while
the "cuffs" around the arm slits get
the stockinette treatment.

BODY

With circular needles, cast on 90 (106) sts. Work
back and forth in k2, p2 rib for 5½"/14cm, inc 5
sts evenly across last RS row—95 (111) sts. Work
in trinity st until piece measures 12"/30.5cm
from beg, end with a pat row 4.

Divide for armhole openings

Next row (Pat row 1–WS) Work across 10 (14) sts
for left front panel, join 2nd ball of yarn and work
across 75 (83) sts for 2nd half of left front, back
and first part of right front, join a 3rd ball of yarn,
work to end for right front panel.

Next row (RS) P to last st of first section, inc 1 st
(for selvage); on next section, inc 1 st (for
selvage), p to last st of center section, inc 1 st
(for selvage); on last section, inc 1 st (for
selvage), p to end. Cont to work each section
with separate balls of yarn (working either all 3
sections at one time or each section separately)
for 6 (7½)"/15.5cm (19)cm, keeping the k1
selvage at the armholes, end with a pat row 3.

Joining row (RS) P9 (13), p3tog, work to last 2 sts
of center panel, p3tog, p to end—95 (111) sts. Cut
all extra balls of yarn and cont trinity st over all
sts for 6½"/16.5cm more, end with a pat row 4.

Neck shaping

Dec row 1 (WS) K2, [SKP] twice, work to last 6 st,

[k2tog] twice, k2—89 (105) sts. P 1 row.

Dec row 2 *K2, [SKP] twice, p2tog, work to last 8 sts, p2tog, [k2tog] twice, k2—85 (101) sts. P 1 row. Rep last 2 rows 3 times more, then rep dec row 2 once more—69 (85) sts

Next (dec) row (RS) P2, [p2tog] twice, p to last 6 sts, [p2tog] twice, p2—65 (81) sts.

Next (dec) row K2, [SKP] twice, k1, work to last 7 sts, k1, [k2tog] twice, k2—59 (75) sts.

Next (dec) row P2, [p2tog] twice, p2tog, p to last 6 sts, [p2tog] twice, p2—55 (71) sts.

Next (dec) row K2, [SKP] twice, k2, work to last 8 sts, k2, [k2tog] twice, k2—49 (65) sts. For size X-Large–2X only, rep last 4 rows once more—(55) sts. Bind off rem 49 (55) sts purlwise.

Neckband

With RS facing and circular needle, beg at lower right front edge, pick up and k 133 (141) sts evenly along right front, back neck and left front edge.

Row 1 (RS) *K1, p1; rep from *, end k1. Rep row 1 for seed st for 6"/15cm. Bind off in pat.

Armhole opening border

With RS facing and dpn, pick up and k 24 (30) sts evenly around each armhole opening. Join and work in St st for 2"/5cm. Bind off loosely. ✢

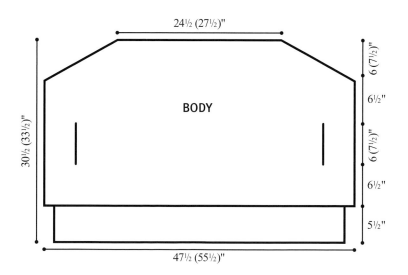

Wavy Lace Wrap

As sensuous as can be, Deborah Newton's lace mantle is knit in 100 percent cashmere. The main section features a wavy lace pattern, while the borders are knit in a more geometric scheme.

■■■▢

KNITTED MEASUREMENTS

Approx 21" x 72"/53cm x 183cm

MATERIALS

13 1¾ oz/50g hanks (each approx 125yd/114m) of Plymouth Yarn Company *Royal Cashmere* (fine cashmere) in #4270 olive green (4)

One pair size 8 (5mm) needles OR SIZE TO OBTAIN GAUGE

Stitch markers

GAUGE

20 sts and 26 rows = 4"/10cm over wavy lace pat using size 8 (5mm) needles.

TAKE TIME TO CHECK GAUGE.

NOTE

Work first 2 and last 2 sts in St st (edge sts).

WAVY LACE PATTERN

(multiple of 11 sts plus 1)

Row 1 and all WS rows K1, *p10, k1; rep from * to end.

Rows 2 and 4 P1, *k10, p1; rep from * to end.

Rows 6, 10 and 14 P1, *k1, [yo, k1] 3 times, ssk 3 times, p1; rep from * to end.

Rows 8 and 12 P1, *k1, [k1, yo] 3 times, ssk 3 times, p1; rep from * to end.

Rows 16 and 18 Rep rows 2 and 4.

Rows 20, 24 and 28 P1, *[k2tog] 3 times, [k1, yo] 3 times, k1, p1; rep from * to end.

Rows 22 and 26 P1, *[k2tog] 3 times, [yo, k1] 3 times, k1, p1; rep from * to end.

Rep rows 1–28 for wavy lace pat.

LACE BORDER PATTERN

(multiple of 10 sts plus 4)

Row 1 (WS) Purl.

Row 2 K2, *yo, ssk, k8; rep from *, end k2.

Row 3 K2, *yo, p2tog, p5, p2tog tbl, yo, p1; rep from *, end k2.

Row 4 K4, *yo, ssk, k3, k2tog, yo, k3; rep from * to end.

Row 5 K2, p2, *yo, p2tog, p1, p2tog tbl, yo, p5; rep from *, end last rep p3, k2.

Row 6 K6, *yo, SK2P, yo, k7; rep from *, end last rep k5.

Row 7 K2, *p3, p2tog tbl, yo; rep from *, end k2.

Row 8 K3, *yo, ssk, k3; rep from *, end k1.

Row 9 K2, p1, *p2tog tbl, yo, p3; rep from *, end last rep p2, k2.

Row 10 K5, *yo, ssk, k3; rep from *, end last rep k2.

Row 11 K1, *p2tog tbl, yo, p3; rep from *, end p1, k2.

Row 12 K2, *yo, ssk, k3; rep from *, end k2.

Rows 13, 14, 15 and 16 Rep rows 3, 4, 5 and 6.

Row 17 K2, p1, *p3, yo, p2tog; rep from *, end k1.

Row 18 K5, *k2tog, yo, k3; rep from *, end last rep k2.

Row 19 K2, p1, *yo, p2tog, p3; rep from *, end last rep p2, k2.

Row 20 K3, *k2tog, yo, k3; rep from *, end k1.

Row 21 K2, *p3, yo, p2tog; rep from *, end k2.

Row 22 K1, *k2tog, yo, k3; rep from *, end k3.

Rows 23, 24, 25 and 26 Rep rows 3, 4, 5 and 6.

Row 27 Purl. These 27 rows form lace border pat.

WRAP

Cast on 104 sts.

Preparation row (RS) K2 (edge sts), p1, *k10, p1; rep from * to last 2 sts, k2 (edge sts).

Next row (WS) P2 (edge sts), work row 1 of wavy lace pat over 100 sts, end p2 (edge sts). Cont in wavy lace pat, keeping first and last 2 sts in St st, until piece measures 64"/162.5cm, end with a row 5 or 19. Bind off loosely.

BORDERS

With RS facing, pick up and k 100 sts evenly along bound-off edge.

Row 1 (WS) P2, k1 (edge sts), k to last 3 sts, k1, p2 (edge sts).

Row 2 K2, p1 (edge sts), k to last 3 sts, p1, k2 (edge sts). Rep last 2 rows once more.

Next row (WS) P2, k1, work row 1 of lace border pat over 94 sts, k1, p2. Cont as established, working first and last 3 sts as edge sts, until 27 rows of lace border pat complete.

Next row (RS) K2, p1 (edge sts), k to last 3 sts, p1, k2 (edge sts).

Next row P2, k1 (edge sts), k to last 3 sts, k1, p2 (edge sts).

Rep last 2 rows once more. Bind off loosely. Rep border along cast-on edge. ✛

Wide Rib Shrug

■□□▭

KNITTED MEASUREMENTS

Width (slightly stretched) approx 36 (41½)"/91.5 (105.5)cm

Length (folded) 10 (11)"/25.5 (28)cm

MATERIALS

Original Yarn

4 (5) 3½oz/100g balls (each approx 60yd/55m) of Tahki Yarns/Tahki•Stacy Charles, Inc., *Baby* (wool) in #18 brown 〔4〕

Substitute Yarn

4 (5) 1¾oz/50g balls (each approx 63yd/58m) of GGH/Muench Yarns *Aspen* (merino wool/polyacrylic) in #31 khaki 〔6〕

Size 13 (9mm) circular needle, 24"/60cm or 32"/80cm long OR SIZE TO OBTAIN GAUGE

GAUGE

10 sts and 13 rnds = 4"/10cm over k4, p4 rib (slightly stretched) using size 13 (9mm) needles. TAKE TIME TO CHECK GAUGE.

NOTES

1) If necessary, to make edges looser, use one size larger needle to cast on and bind off.

2) To make shrug wider or narrower, simply add or subtract 8 sts to cast-on. Be sure to adjust yarn amounts if changing dimensions.

Rosemary Drysdale's super-simple shoulder-hugging shrug is worded in the round in a wide rib pattern. It's a no-fuss project: no shaping or finishing required.

SHRUG

Cast on 88 (104) sts. Join, taking care not to twist sts on needle. Place a marker for end of rnd and slip marker every rnd.

Rnd 1 *K4, p4; rep from * around. Rep rnd 1 for rib until piece measures 14 (15)"/35.5 (38)cm from beg, or 4"/10cm less than desired length. Bind off loosely in rib.

FINISHING

Fold 4"/10cm from bound-off edge to RS. ✛

Fringed Wrap

A sumptuous wrap is just the thing for days when a jacket is too much. Sandi Prosser's seed stitch example is knit on big needles and trimmed with I-cord fringe.

■■□□

KNITTED MEASUREMENTS

Approx 18" x 85"/45.5cm x 216cm (without fringe)

MATERIALS

Original Yarn

18 1¾oz/50g balls (each approx 82yd/75m) of Needful Yarns *Orsetto* (wool/polyamide) in #102 light blue 🟦5

Substitute Yarn

14 1¾oz/50g balls (each approx 109yd/99m) of Knit One, Crochet Too, Inc. *Fleece* (polyester) in #602 sky blue 🟦6

One pair size 13 (9mm) needles OR SIZE TO OBTAIN GAUGE

Two size 10½ (6.5mm) dpn

Stitch holder

GAUGE

7.5 sts and 15 rows = 4"/10cm over seed st using 2 strands of yarn held tog and size 13 (9mm) needles.

TAKE TIME TO CHECK GAUGE.

NOTE

Use 2 strands of yarn held tog for shawl, and 1 strand for fringe.

SEED STITCH

Row 1 (RS) *K1, p1; rep from * to end.

Row 2 K the purl sts and p the knit sts.

Rep row 2 for seed st.

I-CORD FRINGE (make 17)

With one strand of yarn and dpn, cast on 4 sts.

Next (I-cord) row (RS) *K4, do not turn. Slide sts back to beg of needle to work next row from RS; rep from * until I-cord measures 10"/25.5cm. Cut yarn. Place sts on holder.

SHAWL

With 2 strands of yarn and larger needles, work I-cords from holder as foll: K2tog twice across each I-cord—34 sts. Work in seed st for 85"/216cm.

I-CORD FRINGE

**With one strand of yarn and dpn, inc 1 st in both first and second sts. Do not turn. Slide sts back to beg of needle to work next row from RS. Work I-cord row as above until I-cord measures 10"/25.5cm. Bind off. Rejoin yarn and rep from ** until 17 I-cords have been completed.

FINISHING

Block to measurements. ✥

■■■▢

KNITTED MEASUREMENTS

Depth of wrap 25"/63.5cm

Length of wrap 78"/198cm

Upper arm 14"/35.5cm

MATERIALS

Original Yarn

21 1¾oz/50g balls (each approx 55yd/50m) of Lion Brand Yarn *Kool Wool* (wool/acrylic) in #098 ecru (A) ⬤3

15 1½oz/40g balls (each approx 57yd/52m) of Lion Brand Yarn *Fun Fur Prints* (polyester) in #205 sandstone (B) ⬤5

Substitute Yarn

8 5oz/140g balls (each approx 153yd/140m) of Lion Brand Yarn *Wool-Ease Chunky* (acrylic/wool) in #99 fisherman (A) ⬤5

15 1½oz/40g balls (each approx 57yd/52m) of Lion Brand Yarn *Fun Fur Prints* (polyester) in #205 sandstone (B) ⬤5 (same as original yarn)

One pair size 11 (8mm) needles OR SIZE TO OBTAIN GAUGE

One size 9 (5.5mm) circular needle, 16"/40cm long

GAUGES

11 sts and 15 rows = 4"/10cm over woven pat st using A and B with size 11 (8mm) needles

15 sts and 19 rows = 4"/10cm over k1, p1 rib (slightly stretched) using A and size 9 (5.5mm) needles.

TAKE TIME TO CHECK GAUGES.

WOVEN PATTERN STITCH

NOTE When working with A, always work with 1 strand A. When working with B, always work with

Furry Wrap

With deceptively simple stitchery, Vladimir Teriokhin adds sleeves to a furry wrap. The look is fun and functional— no slipping off the shoulders.

2 strands B (when 2 stands of B are at front of work, they are carried across 3 B knit or purl sts).

Row 1 (RS) With 1A and 2B, k1, p1, k1, p1 (for 4-st band); then cont in woven pat st, with 2 strands B at front of work, k1 with A, *then combine 1 strand A with 2 strands B and k1; with 2 strands B at front of work, k3 with A, bring 2A to back of work; rep from *, end k1 with 1 strand A and 2 strands B; then cont with 1A and 2B, p1, k1, p1, k1 (for 4-st band).

Row 2 With 1A and 2B, k2, p1, k1 (for 4-st band); then cont in woven pat st, with 2 strands B at front (on the RS of work), p2 with A, *then cont 1 strand A with 2 strands B and p1; with 2 strands B at front (RS) of work, p3 with A, bring 2A to back of work; rep from * end with 2A at RS, p3 with A; then cont with 1 A and 2B, k1, p1, k2 (for 4-st band). Rep rows 1 and 2 for woven pat st with 4-st bands.

WRAP

Beg at side edge of wrap with size 11 (8mm) needles and A, cast on 71 sts.

Row 1 (RS) With 1A and 2B, k1, p1, k1, p1 (4-st band); then cont in woven rib pat, with 2 strands A at front of work, k1 with A, *then combine 1 strand A with 2B and p1; with 2 strands B at front of work, (k1, p1, k1) with A; rep from * end p1 with 1A and 2B, k1 with A and with 2 strands B at

front, then with 1A and 2B, p1, k1, p1, k1 (4-st band).

Row 2 (WS) With 1A and 2B, k2, p1, k1 (4-st band), then cont in woven rib pat, with 2 strands B at front (on the RS of work), (p1, k1, p1) with A, *then combine 1 strand A with 2 strands B and k1, with 2 strands B at front (RS) of work, (p1, k1, p1) with A; rep from *, end cont with 1A and 2 B, k1, p1, k2 (4-st band). Rep these 2 rows for woven rib pat until piece measures 3"/7.5cm from beg. Then cont in woven pat st until piece measures 31½"/80cm from beg.

Opening for left sleeve

Row 1 (RS) Work 28 sts in woven pat st, bind off next 27 sts using A only, work rem 16 sts in woven pat st.

Row 2 (WS) Work to bound-off sts, cast on 21 sts to replace the bound-off sts, work to end. Work even on all sts for 15"/38cm more OR until piece measures approx 46½"/118cm from beg, end with a WS row. Rep rows 1 and 2 of opening for sleeve (for right sleeve opening). Then cont in woven pat st on all sts until piece measures 75"/190.5cm from beg. Work in woven rib pat as for beg of wrap for 3"/7.5cm. Bind with A only in rib.

SLEEVES

Picking up sts around one sleeve opening (so that seam of sleeve is at the beg of the wider or 26-st end) with smaller needle and A, pick up and k 55 sts evenly around armhole opening. Work in k1, p1 rib for 3"/7.5cm. Dec 1 st each side of next row then every 6th row 11 times more—31 sts.

Work even until sleeve measures 19"/48cm from pick-up. Bind off in rib.

FINISHING

Sew sleeve seams. Omitting ribs, block very lightly, if necessary. ✛

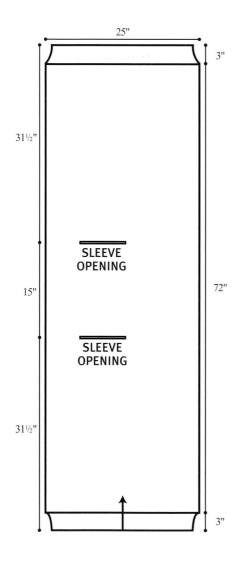

Lace Cape

Designer Pierrot credits the fabulously feminine styles his mother once wore as inspiration for his strict-but-sexy garments, like this lacy pink cape. The lace pattern is reminiscent of vintage lace from the early twentieth century, and the soft pink shade is ultra feminine.

KNITTED MEASUREMENTS
Lower edge (around) 72"/183cm
Length 31"/78.5cm

MATERIALS
18 1¾oz/50g balls (each approx 55yd/50m) of Knit One, Crochet Too, Inc. *Temptation* (baby alpaca/merino wool) in #212 soft sunrise ⑤
One pair size 11 (8mm) needles OR SIZE TO OBTAIN GAUGE
Stitch markers

GAUGES
34 sts = 9" in lace pat using size 11 (8mm) needles
12 sts and 20 rows = 4" over beaded rib pat using size 11 (8mm) needles.
TAKE TIME TO CHECK GAUGES.

LACE PATTERN
(multiple of 34 sts plus 2)
Row 1 (RS) K1, *yo, ssk, k2, yo, ssk, p2, yo, k4, ssk, k6, k2tog, k4, yo, p2, k2, yo, ssk, k2; rep from *, end k1.
Row 2 K1, *yo, p2tog, p2, yo, p2tog, k2, p1, yo, p4, p2tog, p4, p2tog tbl, p4, yo, p1, k2, p2, yo, p2tog, p2; rep from *, end k1.
Row 3 K1, *yo, ssk, k2, yo, ssk, p2, k2, yo, k4, ssk, k2, k2tog, k4, yo, k2, p2, k2, yo, ssk, k2; rep from *, end k1.
Row 4 K1, *yo, p2tog, p2, yo, p2tog, k2, p3, yo, p4, p2tog, p2tog tbl, p4, yo, p3, k2, p2, yo, p2tog, p2; rep from *, end k1.
Rows 5–12 Rep rows 1-4 twice more.
Row 13 (RS) K1, *k3, k2tog, k4, yo, p2, [k2, yo, ssk] 3 times, p2, yo, k4, ssk, k3; rep from *, end k1.

Row 14 K1, *p2, p2tog tbl, p4, yo, p1, k2, [p2, yo, p2tog] 3 times, k2, p1, yo, p4, p2tog, p2; rep from *, end k1.

Row 15 K1, *k1, k2tog, k4, yo, k2, p2, [k2, yo, ssk] 3 times, p2, k2, yo, k4, ssk, k1; rep from *, end k1.

Row 16 K1, *p2tog tbl, p4, yo, p3, k2, [p2, yo, p2tog] 3 times, k2, p3, yo, p4, p2tog; rep from *, end k1.

Rows 17–24 Rep rows 13–16 twice more.

Rep rows 1–24 for lace pat.

BEADED RIB

Row 1 (RS) Sl 1, p to end.

Row 2 Sl 1, *k1, p1; rep from * to end.

Rep rows 1 and 2 for beaded rib.

CAPE

Cast on 274 sts. Work in lace pat for 48 rows.

Beg shaping

Next row (RS) Work 73 sts, (do not work last yo), k3tog, place marker, SK2P (sl 1, k2tog, psso), work 116 sts, k3tog, place marker, SK2P, (do not work next yo), work to end.

Cont in this way to dec 2 sts each side of both markers (working dec sts into lace pat) every

4th row 4 times more, every other row 20 times—74 sts.

Work even until 108 rows have been worked from beg. Piece measures approx 31"/78.5 from beg. Bind off all sts.

COLLAR

Cast on 119 sts. Work in beaded rib, dec 1 st each side (1 st in from edge) every 4th row 6 times—107 sts.

Work even until collar measures 7½"/19cm. Bind off. Beg at 2"/5cm in from each front neck edge, sew bound-off edge of collar around neck. ✣

Bobble Trim Wrap

Contrasting bobble trim knit on either end of the piece adds a fun accent to Linda Cyr's fluted-rib rectangular wrap.

■■□□

KNITTED MEASUREMENTS

18" x 72"/46cm x 183cm

MATERIALS

• 11 1¾oz/50g balls (each approx 102yd/93m) Plymouth Yarns *Baby Alpaca Worsted* (baby alpaca) in #208 camel (MC) **4**
• 1 ball in #500 black (CC)
• Size 7 (4.5mm) circular needle 24"/61cm long OR SIZE TO OBTAIN GAUGE
• Size G (4.5mm) crochet hook

NOTE

Always start a new skein of yarn at beg of row.

GAUGE

18 sts and 24 rows = 4"/10cm in St st (check gauge in St st as pat st falls into pleats) using size 7(4.5mm) needles.
TAKE TIME TO CHECK GAUGE.

STITCH GLOSSARY

Bobble (MB)

[K1, p1, k1, p1, k1] in one st, turn. Work 7 rows garter st over 5 sts.

Next row Sl 3 sts knitwise, k3tog tbl, place st on LH needle, k3tog, place st on LH needle. Insert RH needle into base of bobble (original first st), psso st on LH needle.

FLUTED RIB (multiple of 8 sts plus 1)

Rows 1–3 P1, *k1, p1; rep from * to end.

Row 4 K2, *p5, k3; rep from *, end p5, k2.
Row 5 P3, *k3, p5; rep from *, end k3, p3.
Row 6–8 K4, *p1, k7; rep from *, end p1, k4.
Row 9 Rep row 5.
Row 10 Rep row 4. Rep rows 1–10 for pat.

WRAP

With CC, cast on 97 sts.
Row 1 *Make bobble (MB), k7; rep from *, end MB.
Rows 2 and 3 Knit.
Row 4 Change to MC, *k1, p1; rep from *, end k1. Beg fluted rib pat, cont until piece measures 70"/178cm from beg, end with a WS row.
Next row Change to CC (do not cut MC), *k1, p1; rep from *, end k1. Knit the next 2 rows.
Next row *MB, k1, psso (counts as first bind-off), bind off 7 more sts; rep from *, end MB. Cut CC yarn, pull through.

FINISHING

Pick up MC, with crochet hook, work 1 row of rev sc along side edge, fasten off. Rep for other side. Block lightly. ✤

Fringed Stole With Pockets

Lipp Holmfeld's stylish seed stitch block stole is simply a long rectangle finished with fringe. The front edge is folded back and stitched down; the openings create two cozy pockets.

◼◼☐☐

KNITTED MEASUREMENTS

Approx 68" x 22"/172.5cm x 56cm (before foldback)

MATERIALS

17 1¾ oz/50g balls (each approx 55yd/50m) of Dale of Norway *Ara* (wool) in #23063 red mix (5)

One pair size 10 (6mm) needles OR SIZE TO OBTAIN GAUGE

Size H/8 (5mm) crochet hook

GAUGE

14 sts and 24 rows = 4"/10cm over stitch pat using size 10 (6mm) needles.

TAKE TIME TO CHECK GAUGE.

STITCH PATTERN

Rows 1 3, 5, 7, 9, 11 (RS) Sl 1 purlwise, k3 (front edge), [k1, p1] 5 times, p2, *k1, p1; rep from * to end.

Rows 2, 4, 6, 8, 10, 12 Sl 1 purlwise, *[k1, p1] 4 times, p2; rep from * 4 times more, **k1, p1; rep from ** to last 3 sts, p3.

Row 13 (RS) Knit.

Row 14 K to last 3 sts, p3.

Rep these 14 rows for st pat.

STOLE

Cast on 74 sts. Work in st pat until piece measures approx 68"/172.5cm, bind off on row 13.

FINISHING

Fold front edge with 4 k sts to RS to cover 2 panels, creating stole with 3 single layer panels and 2 double layer panels. Sew edge down for 5"/12.5cm (approx 2 rep's of pat), leave next 5"/12.5cm unsewn for pocket, cont to sew to last 10"/25.5 and form 2nd pocket.

Steam lightly. ✢

KNITTED MEASUREMENTS

Approx 22½"/57cm wide by 72"/183cm long

MATERIALS

Original Yarn

12 1¾oz/50g balls (each approx 192yd/177m) of Filatura Di Crosa/Stacy Charles Collection *Butterfly* (mohair/acrylic) in #400 white ▣

Substitute Yarn

9 .88oz/25g balls (each approx 269yd/245m) of Filatura Di Crosa/Tahki•Stacy Charles, Inc. *Baby Kid Extra* (super kid mohair/nylon) in #301 off white ▣

One pair each sizes 7 and 9 (4.5mm and 5.5mm) needles OR SIZE TO OBTAIN GAUGE
Cable needle
Stitch markers

GAUGE

32 sts and 20 rows = 4"/10cm (blocked) over chart pat using larger needles. TAKE TIME TO CHECK GAUGE.

STITCH GLOSSARY

24-st LC

Sl 12 sts to cn and hold to *front,* [k2, p2] 3 times,

Cabled Rib Shawl

Lily Chin's reversible cabled-rib shawl is the ultimate indulgence in a super-soft mohair blend.

work sts from cn as foll: [k2, p2] 3 times.

24-st RC

Sl 12 sts to cn and hold to *back,* [k2, p2] 3 times, work sts from cn as foll: [k2, p2] 3 times.

BACK

With smaller needles, cast on 176 sts.

Beg chart pat

Row 1 (RS) K4, pm, work sts 1 to 48 of chart 3 times, then sts 1 to 24 once more, pm, k4.

Row 2 Sl 1 wyif, k3, sl marker, work chart pat to last 4 sts, k3, sl 1 wyif.

Cont in this way for 5 more rows, working first and last 4 sts in garter and sl st pat as established. Change to larger needles, and work even until 70½"/179cm from beg. Change to smaller needles, work even for 7 rows more. Bind off tightly in rib.

FINISHING

Block lightly. ✤

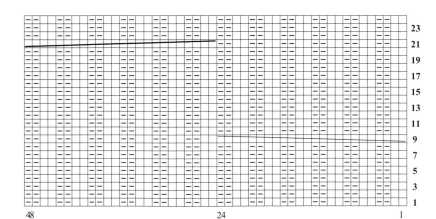

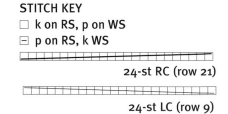

STITCH KEY
☐ k on RS, p on WS
⊟ p on RS, k WS

24-st RC (row 21)

24-st LC (row 9)

■■■▶

KNITTED MEASUREMENTS

Approx 140" x 18"/355.5cm x 45.5cm

MATERIALS

20 3½ oz/100g hanks (each approx 45yd/41m)
of Blue Sky Alpacas *Bulky* (alpaca/wool) in #1211
frost ❻
One pair size 19 (15mm) needles OR SIZE TO
OBTAIN GAUGE

GAUGE

6¼ sts and 9 rows = 4"/10cm over chart pat using
size 19 (15mm) needles and 2 strands held tog.
TAKE TIME TO CHECK GAUGE.

NOTE

Stitch counts increase from 24 to 26 to 28 sts
and decrease again, as indicated on chart.

Leaf Lace Shawl

Bulky alpaca yarn flowers spectacularly
into a huge and stunning wrap when
held double. Designer Tanis Gray went
to extra-long lengths, repeating
the 24-row leaf lace pattern ten
times, but you can easily adjust the
pattern to any length. And you can
use any weight of yarn for an
equally gorgeous effect.

SCARF

With 2 strands of yarn held tog, cast on 24 sts.
Work set-up row of chart on WS. Rep rows
1–24 of chart 10 times, or for desired length.
Bind off. ✣

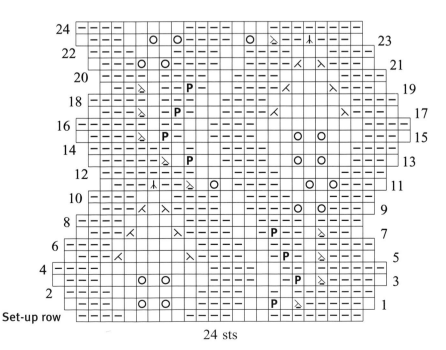

24 sts

STITCH KEY

☐ k on RS, p on WS

▭ p on RS, k on WS

Ⓞ yo

╱ k2tog

╲ ssk

P m1 p-st

⊿ p2tog

⅄ S2KP

All That

Metallic yarns, sparkling
beads, luxury yarns...
these glamorous designs
light up the night.

Glitters

KNITTED MEASUREMENTS

72" x 15"/182.5cm x 38 cm

MATERIALS

6 3½oz/100g hanks (each approx 125yd/114m) of Tilli Tomas *Rock Star* (spun silk and glass beads) in rattan (4)

1 3½oz/100g hank (each approx 260yd/238m) of Tilli Tomas *Pure & Simple* (spun silk) in rattan (4)

One pair size 9 (5.5mm) needles OR SIZE TO OBTAIN GAUGE

Crochet hook for fringe

GAUGE

21 sts and 25 rows = 4"/10cm over pat st using size 9 (5.5mm) needles and *Rock Star*.
TAKE TIME TO CHECK GAUGE.

NOTE

Join new yarn on a k or p row after or before the k3 at each end of the row.

PATTERN STITCH

Row 1 (RS) K3, *k2tog, yo; rep from * to last 3 sts, k3.

Row 2 and all WS rows K3, p to last 3 sts, k3.

Row 3 and 7 Knit.

Row 5 K3, *yo, k2tog; rep from * to last 3 sts, k3.

Row 8 Rep row 2.

Rep rows 1–8 for pat st.

Beaded Stole

Extra-long fringe adds a luxurious note to Rosemary Drysdale's easy allover-lace shawl knit in beaded and silk yarns.

SCARF

With *Rock Star,* cast on 60 sts. Knit 2 rows. Work in pat st until piece measures 72"/182.5cm from beg, or desired length. K 2 rows. Bind off.

Add fringe

Cut 328 strands of *Pure & Simple*, each approx 20"/51cm long. Holding 6 strands tog folded in half, with crochet hook, pull loop through yo at bottom or top of scarf. Wrap around cast-on or bound-off edge and pull ends through loop. Rep for each yo at bottom and top edges of scarf as well as 1 in each k3 section at beg and end of row—29 fringe on each edge. ✛

KNITTED MEASUREMENTS

Approx 14¼" x 76¾"/36cm x 195cm

MATERIALS

8 1¾oz/50g balls (each approx 137yd/125m)
of Debbie Bliss/KFI *Baby Cashmerino* (merino
wool/microfiber/cashmere) in #101
off-white **③**
One pair size 3 (3.25mm) needles OR SIZE TO
OBTAIN GAUGE
1,500 black glass beads

GAUGE

25 sts and 34 rows = 4"/10cm over St st using
size 3 (3.25mm) needles.
TAKE TIME TO CHECK GAUGE.

B1

Bead 1 st by bringing yarn to front of work, slide
bead into position, p1, bring yarn to back of
work, k next st.

PATTERN STITCH

Row 1 (RS) Knit.

Row 2 K1, p to last st, k1.

Row 3 K1, p1, k to last 2 sts, p1, k1.

Row 4 K1, p1, k1, p to last 3 sts, k1, p1, k1.

Row 5 [K1, p1] twice, k to last 4 sts, [p1, k1] twice.

Row 6 K1, [p1, k1] twice, p to last 5 sts, [k1, p1]
twice, k1.

Row 7 Rep row 5.

Row 8 Rep row 4.

Row 9 Rep row 3.

Rep rows 2–9 for pat st.

Beaded Wrap

Delicate knit-in beads in a zigzag
pattern elegantly embellish the ends
of Debbie Bliss's simple rectangular
wrap, knit in a luxurious cashmere-
blend yarn. Seed-stitch patterning
decorates the side edges.

NOTES

1) Make sure beads have a center hole large
enough for a double thickness of yarn to pass
through.

2) Each end of scarf requires 732 beads. Thread
beads onto yarn before starting, threading on a
few more beads than are necessary (to allow for
mistakes or damaged beads).

WRAP

Thread approx 750 beads onto one ball of yarn
and slide along the yarn until there is enough
free yarn for cast on. Cast on 91 sts.

Beg chart

Beg with row 1, work 50 rows of chart. Then work
in pat st until piece measures approx 72"/183cm
from beg, end with row 2 of pat st.

Next row (RS) Knit.

Beg chart

Beg with row 50, work backwards from row 50–1.
Bind off. ✤

BEADING CHART

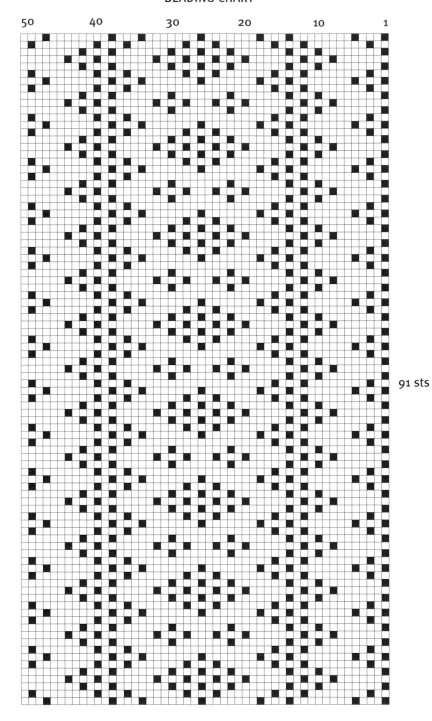

50   40   30   20   10   1

91 sts

STITCH KEY
■ b1, see instructions for beading details
□ k on right side rows and p on wrong side

Diamond Lace Shawl

Created as a rectangle, Barbara Venishnick's gorgeous wrap is a powerful accent piece. It's stitched in an eyelet/diamond pattern and has a knit picot ruffle.

KNITTED MEASUREMENTS
Approx 16" x 80"/40.5cm x 203cm

MATERIALS
Original Yarn
6 4oz/125g hanks (each approx 333yd/300m) of Cherry Tree Hill Yarns *Super Glitz DK* (wool) in wild cherry ③

Substitute Yarn
7 4oz/113g hanks (each approx 313yd/286m) of Cherry Tree Hill Yarns *Silk & Merino DK* (silk/merino) in wild cherry ③
One size 8 (5mm) circular needle, 40"/100cm long OR SIZE TO OBTAIN GAUGE
One size 10 (6mm) circular needle, 40"/100cm long, for cast on only

GAUGE
16 sts and 36 rows = 4"/10cm over diamond pat using size 8 (5mm) needles.
TAKE TIME TO CHECK GAUGE.

DIAMOND PATTERN
(multiple of 16 sts plus 1)
Row 1 (RS) *K6, k2tog, yo, k1, yo, k2tog, k5; rep from *, end k1.
Row 2 and all WS rows Knit.
Row 3 *K5, k2tog, yo, k3, yo, k2tog, k4; rep from *, end k1.
Row 5 *K4, k2tog, yo, k5, yo, k2tog, k3; rep from *, end k1.
Row 7 *K3, k2tog, yo, k7, yo, k2tog, k2; rep from *, end k1.
Row 9 *K2, k2tog, yo, k9, yo, k2tog, k1; rep from *, end k1.

Row 11 *K1, k2tog, yo, k11, yo, k2tog; rep from *, end k1.

Row 13 *K1, yo, k2tog, k11, k2tog, yo; rep from *, end k1.

Row 15 *K2, yo, k2tog, k9, k2tog, yo, k1; rep from *, end k1.

Row 17 *K3, yo, k2tog, k7, k2tog, yo, k2; rep from *, end k1.

Row 19 *K4, yo, k2tog, k5, k2tog, yo, k3; rep from *, end k1.

Row 21 *K5, yo, k2tog, k3, k2tog, yo, k4; rep from *, end k1.

Row 23 *K6, yo, k2tog, k1, k2tog, yo, k5; rep from *, end k1.

Row 24 Knit.

Rep rows 1–24 for diamond pat.

SHAWL

With larger needles, cast on 132 sts, pm, cast on 85 sts, pm, cast on 132 sts—349 sts. Change to smaller needles.

Preparation row (WS) K130, sl 1 wyif, k1, sl marker, k1, sl 1 wyif, k81, sl 1 wyif, k1, sl marker, k1, sl 1 wyif, k130.

Beg diamond pat

Row 1 (RS) K1 (selvage st), work 16-st rep of diamond pat 8 times, end k3, sl marker, k2, work 16-st rep of diamond pat 5 times, end k3, sl marker, k2, work 16-st rep of diamond pat 8 times, end k1, k1 (selvage st).

Row 2 and all WS rows *K to 2 sts before next marker, sl 1 wyif, k1, sl marker, k1, sl 1 wyif; rep from * once more, k to end. Cont in pats as established for 4 rows more.

Dec row (RS) *Work to 3 sts before next marker, k2tog, k1, sl marker, k1, ssk; rep from * once more, work to end. Rep dec row every 6th row 23 times more. Work 24 rows of diamond pat a total of 6 times, then work rows 1 and 2 once more. Bind off rem 253 sts.

Top ruffled edge

With RS facing and smaller needles, pick up and k1 st in every bound-off st at top edge.

Next row K in front and back of each to double sts.

Next row *K2, M1; rep from *, end k2.

Next row *Cast on 4 sts, bind off 5 sts; rep from * until all sts have been worked. Work lower edge in same way.

Left side edge

With RS facing, pick up and k 1 st between each garter ridge (that is 1 st in every other row) along left side edge. Complete as for top edge. Work right side edge in same way. ✤

Felted Shawl

Envelop yourself in a bit of luxury with Deborah Newton's easy, elegant shawl. Stitches are picked up and knit along the outside long edges to keep the piece from pulling in as it felts.

■■☐☐

KNITTED MEASUREMENTS

Approx 24" x 72"/61cm x 183cm (before felting)
Approx 23" x 69"/58cm x 172cm (after felting)

MATERIALS

10 1¾oz/50g hanks (each approx 123yd/112m) of Classic Elite Yarns *Lush* (wool/angora) in #4419 pink icing (4)
One pair size 9 (5.5mm) needles OR SIZE TO OBTAIN GAUGE
Size 10 (6mm) circular needle, 24"/60cm long
Stitch markers

GAUGES

14 sts and 22 rows = 4"/10cm using size 9 (5.5mm) needles (before felting).
16 sts and 24 rows = 4"/10cm using size 9 (5.5mm) needles (after felting).
TAKE TIME TO CHECK GAUGES.

SHAWL

Cast on 84 sts. Work in garter st for 3½"/9cm, place markers after first 12 sts and before last 12 sts on last WS row.
Next row (RS) Work in St st, k12, sl marker, inc 12 sts evenly across next 60 sts to next marker, sl marker, work to end—96 sts. Cont in pat as established, working first and last 12 sts in garter st and center sts in St st until piece measures 68½"/174cm from beg, dec 12 sts evenly between markers on last WS row—84 sts. Work in garter across all sts for 3½"/9cm, end with a WS row. Bind off.

FINISHING

With RS facing and circular needle, pick up and k1 st for each garter ridge along long edge of shawl. K 1 row. Bind off loosely knitwise. Rep on other long edge.

Felting

Set washer for hot wash, longest cycle and lowest water level. Add small amount of mild detergent. Do not use your washer's spin cycle. While agitating, check on the progress every 5 minutes. Set washer back to agitate longer if needed. When the piece is felted to the approx measurements, remove and rinse by hand in cool water. Roll in a towel to remove as much water as possible. ✢

■■■■

KNITTED MEASUREMENTS

24" x 80"/61cm x 201cm

MATERIALS

2 2oz/60g balls (each approx 825yd/754m)
of Jade Sapphire Exotic Fibers *Lacey Lamb*
(lambswool) in #202 pale pink (**1**)
One pair size 5 (3.75mm) knitting needles OR
SIZE TO OBTAIN GAUGE
One size 5 (3.75mm) crochet hook
One 1mm beading crochet hook
1,450 size 6.0 silver lined crystal glass beads
Waste yarn

GAUGE

20 sts and 21 rows = 4"/10cm over body pat.
TAKE TIME TO CHECK GAUGE.

NOTE

You can work from written instructions or from
charts.

STITCH GLOSSARY

AB (add bead)

Sl bead to shank of beading crochet hook. With
hook facing you, sl next st from LH needle onto
crochet hook. Sl bead onto st. Sl st back onto LH
needle and purl.

LS (lace stripe; multiple of 5 sts)

Yo, k2tog, k1, ssk, yo.

Provisional Cast-on

Using waste yarn of a similar weight to the
project yarn and a crochet hook, chain 5 or 6 sts
more than the required cast-on sts. Cut a tail and
pull the tail through the last chain. Using size 5
(3.75mm) needles and the project yarn, pick up

Beaded Lace Shawl

A diaphanous beaded lace shawl by Karen
Joan Raz, worthy of its own standing
ovation, is knit outward from a provisional
cast-on in both directions. Beads are
worked in with the allover lace patterning;
the scalloped points at either short end are
created with a distinct bind-off technique.

the required number of cast-on sts through the
"purl bumps" on the back of the crochet chain.
Be careful not to split the waste yarn, as this
makes it difficult to pull out the crochet chain at
the end. Continue working in pattern as
described. To remove waste chain, pull out the
tail from the last crochet stitch.
Gently and slowly pull on the tail to unravel the
crochet stitches, carefully placing each released
knit stitch on a needle.

SHAWL

Provisionally cast on 120 sts.
Set-up Row 1 (RS) Knit.
Set-up Row 2 (WS) Purl, inc'ing 4 sts evenly
across row—124 sts.
Beg body pat (multiple of 15 sts plus 4)
Row 1 (RS) Ssk, yo, *k3tog, k1, [yo, k1 tbl] 3
times, yo, k1, [ssk] twice, k3; rep from * 7 times
more, yo, k2tog.
Row 2 P2, [p14, AB] 8 times, p2.
Row 3 Ssk, yo, *ssk, k2, yo, k3, yo, k1 tbl, yo, k1,
[ssk] twice, k2; rep from * 7 times more, yo, k2tog.
Row 4 and all WS rows except 2 and 10 (WS) Purl.
Row 5 Ssk, yo, *ssk, k1, yo, k5, yo, k1 tbl, yo, k1,

BODY PATTERN

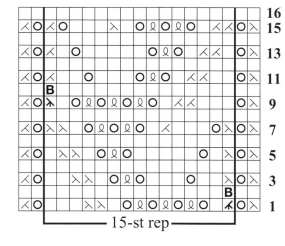

— 15-st rep —

STITCH KEY

☐	k on RS, p on WS
O	yo
ℓ	ktbl
B	add bead (AB)
⟍	ssk
⟋	k2tog
⋏	k3tog
⋋	sssk

LACE EDGE

— LS — 13 sts — LS —

STITCH KEY

☐	k on RS, p on WS
—	p on RS, k on WS
O	yo
B	add bead (AB)
⟍	ssk
⟋	k2tog
⋏	sk2p
⋁	s1 st

[ssk] twice, k1; rep from * 7 times more, yo, k2tog.

Row 7 (RS) Ssk, yo, *ssk, yo, k3, k2tog, k1, [yo, k1 tbl] twice, yo, k1, [ssk] twice; rep from * 7 times more yo, k2tog.

Row 9 Ssk, yo, *k3, [k2tog] twice, k1, [yo, k1 tbl] 3 times, yo, k1, sssk; rep from * 7 times more, yo, k2tog.

Row 10 (WS) P2, [AB, p14] 8 times, p2.

Row 11 Ssk, yo, *k2, [k2tog] twice, k1, yo, k1 tbl, yo, k3, yo, k2, k2tog; rep from * 7 times more, yo k2tog.

Row 13 Ssk, yo, *k1, [k2tog] twice, k1, yo, k1 tbl, yo, k5, yo, k1, k2tog; rep from * 7 times more, yo, k2tog.

Row 15 Ssk, yo, *[k2tog] twice, k1, [yo, k1 tbl] twice, yo, k1, ssk, k3, yo, k2tog; rep from * 7 times more, yo, k2tog.

Row 16 (WS) Purl. Rep rows 1–16 of body pat 21 times more, then work rows 1 and 2 once more.

Set up lace edge

Row 1 (RS) Knit.

Row 2 (WS) Purl, dec'ing 4 sts evenly across row—120 sts.

Lace edge

With RS facing, cast on 30 sts.

Row 1 (RS) Yo, k2tog, k1, yo, k3, LS, [k1, yo, ssk, k1, k2tog, yo] twice, k1, LS, ssk, turn.

Row 2 (WS) Sl 1, p2, AB, p17, [AB, p3] twice, k2.

Row 3 Yo, k2tog, k1, yo, k4, LS, [k1, yo, k1, sk2p, k1, yo] twice, k1, LS, ssk, turn.

Row 4 Sl 1, p2, [AB, p5] 3 times, AB, p4, AB, p3, k2.

Row 5 Yo, k2tog, k1, yo, k2, k2tog, yo, k1, LS, [k1, k2tog, yo, k1, yo, ssk] twice, k1, LS, ssk, turn.

Row 6 Sl 1, p2, AB, p17, AB, p5, AB, p3, k2.

Row 7 Yo, k2tog, k1, yo, k2, k2tog, yo, k2, LS, k2tog, k1, [yo, k1] twice, sk2p, [k1, yo] twice, k1, ssk, LS, ssk, turn.

Row 8 Sl 1, [p2, AB] twice, [p5, AB] twice, p2, AB,

p6, AB, p3, k2.

Row 9 Yo, k2tog, k1, yo, k2, k2tog, yo, k3, LS, [k1, yo, ssk, k1, k2tog, yo] twice, k1, LS, ssk, turn.

Row 10 Sl st, p2, AB, p17, AB, p7, AB, p3, k2.

Row 11 Yo, k2tog, k1, yo, k2, k2tog, yo, k4, LS, [k1, yo, k1, sk2p, k1, yo] twice, k1, LS, ssk, turn.

Row 12 Sl st, p2, AB, [p5, AB]3 times, p8, AB, p3, k2.

Row 13 Yo, k2tog, ssk, yo, ssk, k2, yo, ssk, k2, LS, [k1, k2tog, yo, k1, yo, ssk] twice, k1, LS, ssk, turn.

Row 14 Rep row 10.

Row 15 Yo, k2tog, ssk, yo, ssk, k2, yo, ssk, k1, LS, k2tog, [k1, yo] twice, k1, sk2p, [k1, yo] twice, k1, ssk, LS, ssk, turn.

Row 16 Rep row 8.

Row 17 Yo, k2tog, ssk, yo, ssk, k2, yo, ssk, LS, [k1, yo, ssk, k1, k2tog, yo] twice, k1, LS, ssk, turn.

Row 18 Rep row 6.

Row 19 Yo, k2tog, ssk, yo, ssk, k3, LS, [k1, yo, k1, sk2p, k1, yo] twice, k1, LS, ssk, turn.

Row 20 Rep row 4.

Row 21 Yo, k2tog, ssk, yo, ssk, k2, LS, [k1, k2tog, yo, k1, yo, ssk] twice, k1, LS, ssk, turn.

Row 22 Rep row 2.

Row 23 Yo, k2tog, ssk, yo, ssk, k1, LS, k2tog, [k1, yo] twice, k1, sk2p, [k1, yo] twice, k1, ssk, LS, ssk, turn.

Row 24 Sl 1, [p2, AB] twice, [p5, AB] twice, [p2, AB] twice, p3, p2.

Rep rows 1–24 of lace edge pat 9 times more. Bind off rem sts loosely.

Finish cast-on edge

Remove waste yarn and place provisional cast-on sts on needles.

Rep 24-row lace edge pat as before.

FINISHING

Block gently. ✣

Ruffled Edge Wrap

That's a wrap, kitten—a ruffled garter-stitch topper by Lisa Daehlin, knit using short rows for the flounce along one edge.

◼◼◼▢

KNITTED MEASUREMENTS

Length, non-ruffled edge, 42"/106.5cm

Width 14"/35.5cm

MATERIALS

Original Yarn

4 4oz/113g hanks (each approx 165yd/151m) of Fiesta Yarns Starburst *La Boheme* (kid mohair/rayon/nylon) in #22101 abelone ◼④

Substitute Yarn

4 4oz/113g hanks (each approx 165yd/151m) of Fiesta Yarns *Insignia La Boheme* (rayon boucle/brushed kid mohair/wool/nylon) in vintage rose ◼④

Size 9 (5.5mm) needles OR SIZE TO OBTAIN GAUGE

GAUGE

14 sts and 25 rows = 4"/10cm over garter st.

TAKE TIME TO CHECK GAUGE.

SHORT ROW WRAPPING (wrap and turn—w&t)

Knit side

1) Wyib, sl next st purlwise.

2) Move yarn between the needles to the front.

3) Sl the same st back to LH needle. Turn work, bring yarn to the p side between needles. One st is wrapped.

4) When short rows are completed, work to just before wrapped st, insert RH needle under the wrap and knitwise into the wrapped st, k them together.

Purl side

1) Wyif, sl next st purlwise.

2) Move yarn between the needles to the back.

3) Sl same st back to LH needle. Turn work, bring yarn back to the p side between the needles. One st is wrapped.

4) When short rows are completed, work to just before wrapped st, insert RH needle from behind into the back lp of the wrap and place on LH needle; P wrap tog with st on needle.

WRAP

Cast on 48 sts. Work in garter st for 4 rows.

Work in Short row pat as foll:

Row 1 K3, w&t.

Row 2 K3.

Row 3 K6 (pick up wrap and knit together with stitch), w&t.

Row 4 K6.

Row 5 K9 (pick up wrap and knit together with stitch), w&t.

Row 6 K9.

Row 7 K12 (pick up wrap and knit together with stitch), w&t.

Row 8 K12.

Row 9 K15 (pick up wrap and knit together with stitch), w&t.

Row 10 K15.

Row 11 K18 (pick up wrap and knit together with stitch), w&t.

Row 12 K18.

Row 13 K21 (pick up wrap and knit together with stitch), w&t.

Row 14 K21.

Row 15 K48 (pick up wrap and knit together with stitch).

Rows 16–18 K48.

Rep rows 1–18 until piece measures approx 42"/106.5cm along non-ruffled edge. Bind off. ✦

Knit and Crochet Shawl

Mari Lynn Patrick's creamy, dreamy fringed shawl has a lovely retro feel. The lacy leaf motif that embellishes the top half is knit; the shell pattern on the lower half is crocheted.

■■□□

FINISHED MEASUREMENTS

32"/81cm at top edge x 18"/45.5cm deep, excluding fringe

MATERIALS

4 8oz/227g hanks (each approx 322yd/294m) of Valley Yarns *Monterey* (cotton/wool) in #8179 natural (4)

One pair size 9 (5.5mm needles) OR SIZE TO OBTAIN GAUGE

Size 9 (5.5mm) circular needle, 40"/100cm long

Size I/9 (5.5mm) crochet hook

One 1-inch/25mm button

GAUGES

One 22-st twin leaf panel = 4½"/11.5cm, 20 rows = 4"/10cm over twin leaf (knit) pat foll chart using size 9 (5.5mm) needles.

One shell pat = 3½"/9cm and 10 rows = 4"/10cm over shell (crochet) pat using size I/9 (5.5mm) hook.

TAKE TIME TO CHECK GAUGES.

ABBREVIATION

SSK and Pass Ssk, return the resulting st to LH needle and using RH needle, pass the next st over it and off needle; then sl the st back to RH needle.

TWIN LEAF PANEL (over a panel of 22 sts)

Row 1 and all WS rows P10, k2, p10.

Row 2 K6, ssk and pass, yo, kl, yo, p2, yo, k1, yo, SK2P, k6.

Row 4 K4, ssk and pass, k1 [yo, k1] twice, p2, k1, [yo, k1] twice, SK2P, k4.

Row 6 K2, ssk and pass, k2, yo, k1, yo, k2, p2, k2, yo, k1, yo, k2, SK2P, k2.

Row 8 Ssk and pass, k3, yo, k1, yo, k3, p2, k3, yo, k1, yo, k3, SK2P.

Rep rows 1–8 for twin leaf panel.

SHAWL

Beg at lower edge, cast on 50 sts.

Beg chart pat

Row 1 (WS) K2, work 24-st rep twice. Cont chart in this way, casting on 4 sts at beg of next 14 rows, 2 sts at beg of next 28 rows, 1 st at beg of next 8 rows—170 sts.

Work even through row 57 of chart.

Next row (RS) [K2tog, k2, k2tog, k2, k2tog, k2] 14 times, k2tog—127 sts. K 1 row. P 1 row. Bind off knitwise on WS.

FINISHING

Block shawl flat, being sure not to stretch out the top edge.

Crochet edge

Place a yarn marker to mark center of back at cast-on edge. With size I/9 (5.5mm) crochet hook, working around the curved lower edge of shawl, work 70 sc to marker, pick up 1 st at center, work 70 sc to other edge—141 sc.

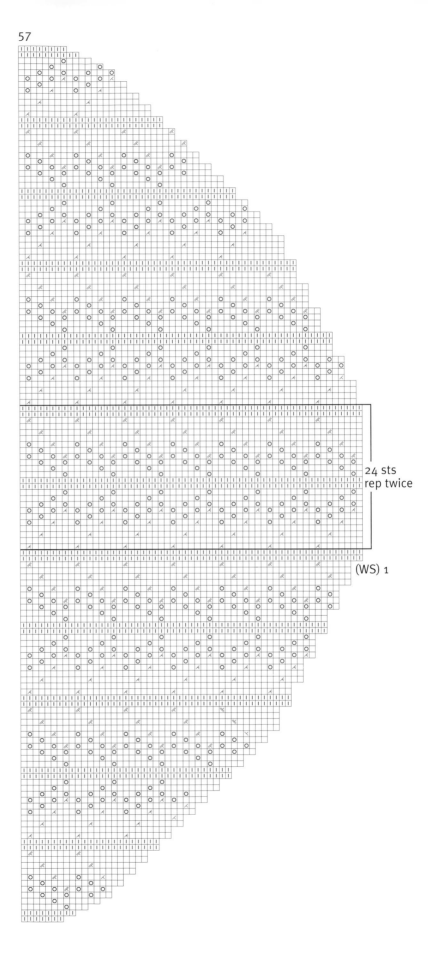

24 sts
rep twice

(WS) 1

STITCH KEY

☐ k on RS, p on WS

⊟ p on RS, k on WS

◎ yo

⊠ SKP

⊠ k2tog

⊠ SK2P

⊠ ssk and pass

Then, ch 7 for buttonloop, and working along the top edge of shawl, just under the purl ridge trim, hold yarn to WS and work "punch" sl st along this row to hold in the edge firmly, to approx 36"/91.5cm. Join with sl st to first sc. From this point on, the crochet edge will be worked around the semicircle lower edge only.

Row 1 (RS) Ch 6, 1 dc in first sc, *ch 3, skip 3 sc, 1 sc in each of next 3 sc, ch 3, skip 3 sc, (1 hdc, ch 3, 1 hdc) in next sc; rep from * to end. Turn.

Row 2 Ch 3, *7 dc in ch-3 loop, ch 3, sc in 2nd of 3 sc, ch 3; rep from *, end 7 dc in last ch-6 loop. Turn.

Row 3 Ch 3 (counts as 1 dc), skip first dc, 1 dc in each of next 6 dc, *ch 3, 1 sc in next sc, ch 3, 1 dc in each of next 7 dc; rep from * to end. Turn.

Row 4 Ch 1, *work 1 sc in each of next 7 dc, ch 5; rep from * end 1 sc in each of last 7 dc. Turn.

Row 5 Ch 5, *sc in each of center 3 dc of 7-dc shell, ch 3, (1 dc, ch 3, 1 dc) in 3rd ch of ch-5, ch 3; rep from *, end sc in each of center 3 dc of 7-dc shell, end ch 5, join with sl st to last sc. Turn.

Row 6 Ch 5, *1 sc in 2nd of 3 sc, ch 3**, 7 dc in ch-3 space between 2 dc, ch 3; rep from *, end last repeat at **, 1 sc in 3rd ch of ch-5 loop. Turn.

Row 7 Ch 5, skip first sc, *1 sc in next sc, ch 3, 1 dc in each of 7 dc, ch 3; rep from *, end 1 sc in sc, ch 3, 1 sc in ch-5 loop. Turn.

Row 8 Ch 6, skip first sc, (1 dc, ch 3, 1 dc) in next sc, *ch 3, skip 2 dc, 1 sc in each of next 3 dc, ch 3, work (1 dc, ch 3, 1 dc) in next sc; rep from *, end dc in 3rd ch of ch-5. Turn. Rep rows 2–7 once.

Last row (RS) Ch 5, sc in first sc, ch 3, *sc in first dc of 7-dc group, ch 3, sc in center dc, ch 3, sc in last dc of 7-dc group, ch 5; rep from *, end ch 3, sc in last sc, ch 3, sc in ch-5 loop; then cont up the side edge, work 21 sc to straighten the knitted edge. Fasten off. Work 21 sc along other front edge in same way.

Fringe

For each fringe, cut six 14"/36cm lengths and place 1 fringe at each scallop center and in center of each ch-5 loop—29 fringes. Sew button at left neck edge to correspond to button loop. ✥

Lacy Leaves Shawl

A rapturous knit shawl by Karen Joan Raz links three panels of a lacy leaf pattern with eyelet sections. Knit in luxurious cashmere, the fabric has beads worked into it with a fine crochet hook. (The lovely colorway, Tanis Grays, is named for our yarn editor.)

KNITTED MEASUREMENTS

Approx 76"/193cm wide at top edge and 29"/73.5 cm deep at center (after blocking).

MATERIALS

3 2oz/55g hanks (each approx 400yd/367m) of Jade Sapphire Exotic Fibres *2-Ply Mongolian Cashmere* (cashmere) in #82 Tanis Grays 🄴
Size 7 (4.5mm) circular needle, 24"/60cm long
Extra size 7 (4.5mm) needles for 3-needle bind-off
One 1mm beading crochet hook
1,400 Size 6/0 silver-lined crystal glass beads

GAUGE

16 sts and 28 rows = 4"/10cm over chart pat, after blocking, using size 7 (4.5mm) needles.
TAKE TIME TO CHECK GAUGE.

STITCH GLOSSARY

AB (add bead)

Slip bead onto shank of beading crochet hook; with hook facing you, sl next st from LH needle onto crochet hook; sl bead onto st; sl st back to LH needle and knit it.

NOTES

1) Only RS rows are shown on chart. Shawl is worked on every RS row as foll: Work chart pat 3 times, end yo, k2tog, k2.

2) Work every WS row as foll: yo, k2tog, k1, then p the purl sts and k the knit sts to the last 3 sts, k3.

SHAWL

Beg at the center and top of shawl, cast on 9 sts and knit 1 row.

Row 1 (RS) [Yo, k2] 4 times, k1—13 sts.

Row 2 (WS) Yo, k2tog, k1, p7, k3.

Row 3 Yo, k2tog, k1, [yo, k1, yo, k2] 3 times, k1—19 sts.

Row 4 Yo, k2tog, k1, p to the last 3 sts, k3.

Row 5 Yo, k2tog, k1, [yo, k3, yo, k2] 3 times, k1—25 sts.

Row 6 Rep row 4.

Row 7 Yo, k2tog, k1, [yo, k5, yo, k2] 3 times, k1—31 sts.

Row 8 Rep row 4.

Beg chart pattern

Row 9 (RS) Work (chart row 9) 3 times, end yo, k2tog, k2—37 sts.

Row 10 (WS) Yo, k2tog, k1, p the purl sts and k the knit sts to the last 3 sts, k3.

Row 11 Work (chart row 11) 3 times, end yo, k2tog, k2—43 sts.

Row 12 Yo, k2tog, k1, p the purl sts and k the knit sts to the last 3 sts, k3. Cont to work in this way through chart row 28—91 sts.

Row 29 *Beg with first st, work across chart row to beg of the rep, work the 18-st rep, work to end of chart row *; rep between *'s twice more, end

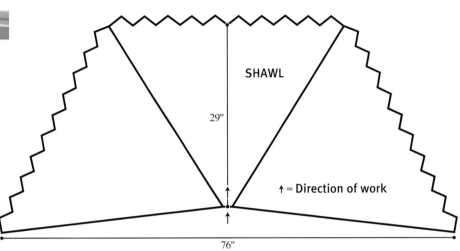

SHAWL

29"

↑ = Direction of work

76"

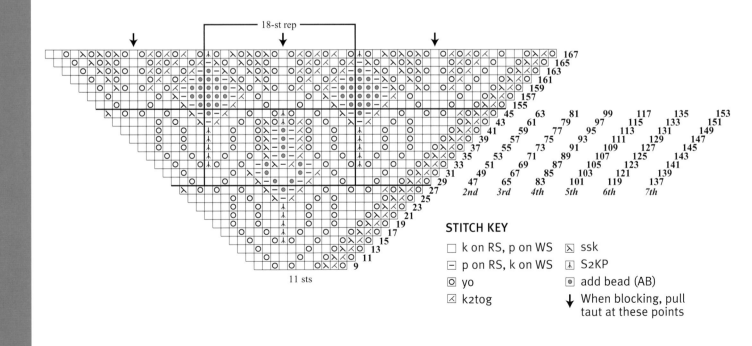

18-st rep

11 sts

STITCH KEY

☐ k on RS, p on WS   ⊠ ssk

⊟ p on RS, k on WS   ⋏ S2KP

◉ yo   ◉ add bead (AB)

⊠ k2tog   ↓ When blocking, pull
taut at these points

yo, k2tog, k2—97 sts.

Cont to foll chart in this way through row 46—145 sts.

Beg the 2nd line of numbers

Row 47 *Beg with first st, work across chart row to beg of rep line, work 18-st rep twice, work to end of chart row *; rep between *'s twice more, end yo, k2tog, k2—151 sts.

Cont to foll chart in this way through row 64—199 sts.

Beg the 3rd line of numbers

Row 65 *Beg with first st, work across chart row to beg of rep line, work 18-st rep 3 times, work to end of chart row *; rep between *'s twice more, end yo, k2tog, k2—205 sts. Cont to foll chart in this way through row 82—253 sts.

Beg the 4th line of numbers

Row 83 *Beg with first st, work across chart row to beg of rep line, work 18-st rep 4 times, work to end of chart row *; rep between *'s twice more, end yo, k2tog, k2—259 sts. Cont to foll chart in this way through row 100—307 sts.

Beg the 5th line of numbers

Row 101 *Beg with first st, work across chart row to beg of rep line, work 18-st rep 5 times, work to end of chart row *; rep between *'s twice more, end yo, k2tog, k2—313 sts. Cont to foll chart in this way through row 118—361 sts.

Beg the 6th line of numbers

Row 119 *Beg with first st, work across chart row to beg of rep line, work 18-st rep 6 times, work to end of chart row *; rep between *'s twice more, end yo, k2tog, k2—367 sts. Cont to foll chart in this way through row 136—415 sts.

Beg the 7th line of numbers

Row 137 *Beg with first st, work across chart row to beg of rep line, work 18-st rep 7 times, work to end of chart row *; rep between *'s twice more, end yo, k2tog, k2—421 sts.

Cont to foll chart in this way through row 154—469 sts.

Row 155 *Beg with first st, work across chart row to beg of rep line, work 18-st rep 8 times, work to end of chart row *; rep between *'s twice more, end yo, k2tog, k2—475 sts.

Cont to foll chart in this way through row 168—511 sts.

This completes the chart pat.

SET UP FOR BINDING OFF

Yo, k2tog, k1, turn, k3. Bind off as foll:

Row 1 (RS) Yo, k2tog, ssk, yo, ssk, turn.

Row 2 (WS) Slip 1, p1, k3.

Rep rows 1 and 2 until 9 sts rem, then:

Row 1 (RS) Yo, k2tog, ssk, yo, ssk, k3—8 sts.

Row 2 (WS) Yo, k2tog, k1, turn.

Row 3 K3.

Row 4 Yo, k2tog, k1, p2, k3. Sl 4 sts to extra needle and place the 2 sets of 4 sts parallel to each other and with RS rows tog. Bind off these sts using 3-needle bind-off.

FINISHING

Block shawl to measurements using wet-block method and pulling out the edge points "taut" as indicated on chart and pinning in place for a saw-tooth edge effect. ✤

KNITTED MEASUREMENTS

15" x 84"/38cm x 213.5cm

MATERIALS

6 .88oz/25g balls (each approx 230yd/210m) of Trendsetter Yarns *Kid Seta* (mohair/silk) in #1015 silver

6 .88oz/25g balls (each approx 200yd/183m) of Lane Borgosesia/Trendsetter Yarns *Toreador* (viscose/polyester) in #101 silver

One pair size 11 (8mm) needles OR SIZE TO OBTAIN GAUGE

Small amount of contrasting scrap yarn

Tapestry needle

GAUGE

15 sts and 20 rows = 4"/10cm over St st using one strand of each yarn held together.

TAKE TIME TO CHECK GAUGE.

TUCK ST

Rows 1, 3 and 5 (RS) Knit.

Rows 2, 4 and 6 Purl. After row 6, thread contrast yarn through sts on needle to mark for pick up later. Do not attach, but leave tail at beg and end of row.

Rows 7, 9 and 11 Knit.

Rows 8 and 10 Purl.

Row 12 (Tuck row) *Lift purl ridge under contrast yarn and put on left needle, p2tog; rep from * to end of row. Remove contrast yarn to use for next repeat. Rep rows 1–12 for Tuck St st.

Tuck Stitch Wrap

Fluid ridges cascade along the length of this ravishing ruffle wrap, secured over one shoulder via a single arm slit. Fayla Reiss knit it in a tucked stockinette stitch, holding together one strand each of two different yarns.

WRAP

With one strand of *Kid Seta* and *Toreador* held together, cast on 42 sts. Work rows 1–12 of Tuck St st once. Cont Tuck St st, inc 1 st at beg of every row 1 on the foll 10 reps—52 sts.

Armhole shaping

At beg of 11th rep, work armhole slit as foll:

Next row Knit 14 sts, bind off next 24 sts, k to end of row.

Next row Purl 14 sts, cast on 24 sts, p to end. Cont in Tuck St st until piece measures 64"/162.5cm from beg. Dec 1 st beg of every row 1 on foll 10 reps—42 sts. Work next rep to row 6 only.

Bind off loosely. ✢

KNITTED MEASUREMENTS

Approx 14" x 83"/35.5cm x 211cm

MATERIALS

10 1¾oz/50g balls (each approx 65yd/60m) of
Classic Elite Yarns *Sinful* (cashmere) in #S20093
natural (5)
One pair size 11 (8mm) needles OR SIZE TO
OBTAIN GAUGE

GAUGE

13 sts and 14 rows = 4"/10cm over eyelet pat
using size 11 (8mm) needles.
TAKE TIME TO CHECK GAUGE.

EYELET PATTERN (over an even number of sts)

Row 1 (RS) K2, *yo, k2tog; rep from * to last 2
sts, k2.
Row 2 K2, p to last 2 sts, k2.
Rep rows 1 and 2 for eyelet pat.

WRAP

Cast on 46 sts. Work in eyelet pat for 83"/211cm,
or desired length. Bind off.

FINISHING

Weave in ends. Block to measurements. ✢

Eyelet Wrap

This openwork mesh-stitch stole
designed by Rosemary Drysdale
drapes you in luxury when worked
in 100 percent cashmere. The
simple stitch pattern is an
easy two-row eyelet that works up
in no time on large needles.

Techniques & Abbreviations

Knitting Needles

U.S.	METRIC
0	2mm
1	2.25mm
2	2.75mm
3	3.25mm
4	3.5mm
5	3.75mm
6	4mm
7	4.5mm
8	5mm
9	5.5mm
10	6mm
10½	6.5mm
11	8mm
13	9mm
15	10mm
17	12.75mm
19	15mm
35	19mm

Crochet Hooks

U.S.	METRIC
B/1	2.25mm
C/2	2.75mm
D/3	3.25mm
E/4	3.5mm
F/5	3.75mm
G/6	4mm
7	4.5mm
H/8	5mm
I/9	5.5mm
J/10	6mm
K/10½	6.5mm
L/11	8mm
M/13	9mm
N/15	10mm

Standard Yarn Weight System

Categories of yarn, gauge ranges, and recommended needle and hook sizes

Yarn Weight Symbol & Category Names	0 Lace	1 Super Fine	2 Fine	3 Light	4 Medium	5 Bulky	6 Super Bulky
Type of Yarns in Category	Fingering 10 count crochet thread	Sock, Fingering, Baby	Sport, Baby	DK, Light Worsted	Worsted, Afghan, Aran	Chunky, Craft, Rug	Bulky, Roving
Knit Gauge Range* in Stockinette Stitch to 4 inches	33–40** sts	27–32 sts	23–26 sts	21–24 sts	16–20 sts	12–15 sts	6–11 sts
Recommended Needle in Metric Size Range	1.5–2.25 mm	2.25–3.25 mm	3.25–3.75 mm	3.75–4.5 mm	4.5–5.5 mm	5.5–8 mm	8 mm and larger
Recommended Needle U.S. Size Range	000 to 1	1 to 3	3 to 5	5 to 7	7 to 9	9 to 11	11 and larger
Crochet Gauge* Ranges in Single Crochet to 4 inch	32-42 double crochets**	21–32 sts	16–20 sts	12–17 sts	11–14 sts	8–11 sts	5–9 sts
Recommended Hook in Metric Size Range	Steel*** 1.6–1.4mm Regular hook 2.25 mm	2.25–3.5 mm	3.5–4.5 mm	4.5–5.5 mm	5.5–6.5 mm	6.5–9 mm	9 mm and larger
Recommended Hook U.S. Size Range	Steel*** 6, 7, 8 Regular hook B–1	B–1 to E–4	E–4 to 7	7 to I–9	I–9 to K–10½	K–10½ to M–13	M–13 and larger

* GUIDELINES ONLY: The above reflect the most commonly used gauges and needle or hook sizes for specific yarn categories.

** Lace weight yarns are usually knitted or crocheted on larger needles and hooks to create lacy, openwork patterns. Accordingly, a gauge range is difficult to determine. Always follow the gauge stated in your pattern.

*** Steel crochet hooks are sized differently from regular hooks--the higher the number, the smaller the hook, which is the reverse of regular hook sizing.

Skill Levels

1. BEGINNER Ideal first project.

2. VERY EASY VERY VOGUE Basic stitches, minimal shaping and simple finishing.

3. INTERMEDIATE For knitters with some experience. More intricate stitches, shaping and finishing.

4. EXPERIENCED For knitters able to work patterns with complicated shaping and finishing.

Basic Stitches

GARTER STITCH Knit every row. Circular knitting: Knit one round, then purl one round.

STOCKINETTE STITCH Knit right-side rows and purl wrong-side rows. Circular knitting: knit all rounds. (U.K.: stocking stitch)

REVERSE-STOCKINETTE STITCH Purl right-side rows and knit wrong-side rows. Circular knitting: purl all rounds. (U.K.: reverse stocking stitch)

Glossary

BIND OFF Used to finish an edge or segment. Lift the first stitch over the second, the second over the third, etc. (U.K.: cast off)

BIND OFF IN RIBBING Work in ribbing as you bind off. (Knit the knit stitches, purl the purl stitches.) (U.K.: cast off in ribbing)

3-NEEDLE BIND-OFF With the right side of the two pieces facing and the needles parallel, insert a third needle into the first stitch on each needle and knit them together. Knit the next two stitches the same way. Slip the first stitch on the third needle over the second stitch and off the needle. Repeat for three-needle bind-off. (See page 140.)

CAST ON Placing a foundation row of stitches upon the needle in order to begin knitting.

DECREASE Reduce the stitches in a row (that is, knit 2 together).

INCREASE Add stitches in a row (that is, knit in front and back of stitch).

KNITWISE Insert the needle into the stitch as if you were going to knit it.

MAKE ONE With the needle tip, lift the strand between the last stitch knit and the next stitch on the left-hand needle and knit into back of it. One knit stitch has been added.

MAKE ONE P-ST With the needle tip, lift the strand between the last stitch worked and the next stitch on the left-hand needle and purl it. One purl stitch has been added.

NO STITCH On some charts, "no stitch" is indicated with shaded spaces where stitches have been decreased or not yet made. In such cases, work the stitches of the chart, skipping over the "no stitch" spaces.

PICK UP AND KNIT (PURL) Knit (or purl) into the loops along an edge.

PLACE MARKERS Place or attach a loop of contrast yarn or purchased stitch marker as indicated.

PURLWISE Insert the needle into the stitch as if you were going to purl it.

SELVAGE STITCH Edge stitch that helps make seaming easier.

SLIP, SLIP, KNIT Slip next two stitches knitwise, one at a time, to right-hand needle. Insert tip of left-hand needle into fronts of these stitches, from left to right. Knit them together. One stitch has been decreased.

SLIP, SLIP, SLIP, KNIT Slip next three stitches knitwise, one at a time, to right-hand needle. Insert tip of left-hand needle into fronts of these stitches, from left to right. Knit them together. Two stitches have been decreased.

SLIP STITCH An unworked stitch made by passing a stitch from the left-hand to the right-hand needle as if to purl.

WORK EVEN Continue in pattern without increasing or decreasing. (U.K.: work straight)

YARN OVER Making a new stitch by wrapping the yarn over the right-hand needle. (U.K.: yfwd, yon, yrn)

Gauge

Make a test swatch at least 4"/10cm square. If the number of stitches and rows does not correspond to the gauge given, you must change the needle size. An easy rule to follow is: To get fewer stitches to the inch/cm, use a larger needle; to get more stitches to the inch/cm, use a smaller needle. Continue to try different needle sizes until you get the same number of stitches in the gauge.

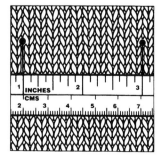

Stitches measured over 2"/5cm.

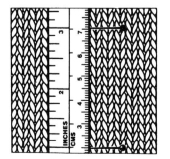

Rows measured over 2"/5cm.

Abbreviations

approx	approximately	**M1 p-st**	make 1 purl stitch (see glossary)	**sl**	slip
beg	begin(ning)			**sl st**	slip stitch (see glossary)
CC	contrasting color	**oz**	ounce(s)	**ssk**	slip, slip, knit (see glossary)
ch	chain	**p**	purl	**sssk**	slip, slip, slip, knit (see glossary)
cm	centimeter(s)	**pat(s)**	pattern(s)		
cn	cable needle	**pm**	place marker (see glossary)	**st(s)**	stitch(es)
cont	continu(e)(ing)	**psso**	pass slip stitch(es) over	**St st**	stockinette stitch
dec	decreas(e)(ing)	**rem**	remain(s)(ing)	**tbl**	through back loop(s)
dpn	double-pointed needle(s)	**rep**	repeat	**tog**	together
foll	follow(s)(ing)	**RH**	right-hand	**WS**	wrong side(s)
g	gram(s)	**RS**	right side(s)	**wyib**	with yarn in back
inc	increas(e)(ing)	**rnd(s)**	round(s)	**wyif**	with yarn in front
k	knit	**SKP**	slip 1, knit 1, pass slip stitch over—one stitch has been decreased	**yd**	yard(s)
LH	left-hand			**yo**	yarn over needle (U.K.: see glossary)
lp(s)	loop(s)	**SK2P**	slip 1, knit 2 together, pass slip stitch over the knit 2 together—two stitches have been decreased	*****	repeat directions following * as many times as indicated
m	meter(s)				
mm	millimeter(s)			**[ ]**	repeat directions inside brackets as many times as indicated
MC	main color	**S2KP**	slip 2 stitches together, knit 1, pass 2 slip stitches over knit 1		
M1	make one (see glossary)				

Knitting Techniques

3-NEEDLE BIND-OFF This bind-off is used to join two edges that have the same number of stitches, such as shoulder edges, which have been placed on holders.

1. With the right side of the two pieces facing each other, and the needles parallel, insert a third needle knitwise into the first stitch of each needle. Wrap the yarn around the needle as if to knit.

2. Knit these two stitches together and slip them off the needles. *Knit the next two stitches together in the same way as shown.

3. Slip the first stitch on the third needle over the second stitch and off the needle. Repeat from the * in step 2 across the row until all the stitches are bound off.

KITCHENER STITCH

1. Insert tapestry needle purlwise (as shown) through first stitch on front needle. Pull yarn through, leaving that stitch on knitting needle.

2. Insert tapestry needle knitwise (as shown) through first stitch on back needle. Pull yarn through, leaving stitch on knitting needle.

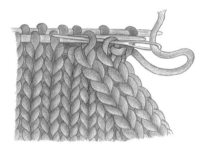

3. Insert tapestry needle knitwise through first stitch on front needle, slip stitch off needle and insert tapestry needle purlwise (as shown) through next stitch on front needle. Pull yarn through, leaving this stitch on needle.

4. Insert tapestry needle purlwise through first stitch on back needle. Slip stitch off needle and insert tapestry needle knitwise (as shown) through next stitch on back needle. Pull yarn through, leaving this stitch on needle.

Repeat steps 3 and 4 until all stitches on both front and back needles have been grafted. Fasten off and weave in end.

DUPLICATE STITCH

Duplicate stitch covers a knit stitch. Bring the needle up below the stitch to be worked. Insert the needle under both loops one row above and pull it through. Insert it back into the stitch below and through the center of the next stitch in one motion, as shown.

FRINGE

Cut yarn twice desired length, plus extra for knotting. On WS, insert hook from front to back through piece and over folded yarn. Pull yarn through. Draw ends through and tighten. Trim yarn.

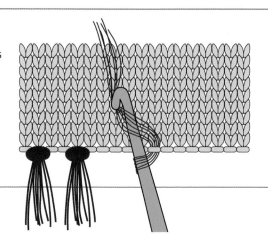

YARN OVERS There are different ways to make a yarn over. Which method to use depends on where you are in the stitch pattern. If you do not make the yarn over in the right way, you may lose it on the following row, or make a yarn over that is too big. Here are some variations:

Between two knit stitches: Bring the yarn from the back of the work to the front between the two needles. Knit the next stitch, bringing the yarn to the back over the right-hand needle, as shown.

Between a knit and a purl stitch: Bring the yarn from the back to the front between the two needles. Then bring it to the back over the right-hand needle and back to the front again, as shown. Purl the next stitch.

Between a purl and a knit stitch: Leave the yarn at the front of the work. Knit the next stitch, bringing the yarn to the back over the right-hand needle, as shown.

Between two purl stitches: Leave the yarn at the front of the work. Bring the yarn to the back over the right-hand needle and to the front again, as shown. Purl the next stitch.

Multiple yarn overs (two or more): Wrap the yarn around the needle, as when working a single yarn over, then continue wrapping the yarn around the needle as many times as indicated. Work the next stitch of the left-hand needle. On the following row, work stitches into the extra yarn overs as described in the pattern. The illustration on the right depicts a finished yarn over on the purl side.

I-CORD Cast on about three to five sitches. *Knit one row. Without turning the work, slip the stitches back to the beginning of the row. Pull the yarn tightly from the end of the row. Repeat from the * as desired. Bind off.

Resources

Berroco, Inc.
P.O. Box 367
14 Elmdale Road
Uxbridge, MA 01569
www.berroco.com

Blue Sky Alpacas
P.O. Box 88
Cedar, MN 55011
www.blueskyalpacas.com

Cherry Tree Hill Yarns
100 Cherry Tree Hill Lane
Barton, VT 05822
www.cherryyarn.com

Classic Elite Yarns
122 Western Avenue
Lowell, MA 01851
www.classiceliteyarns.com

Colinette Yarns
Distributed by
Unique Kolours, Ltd.
www.colinette.com

Crystal Palace Yarns
160 23rd Street
Richmond, CA 94804
www.crystalpalaceyarns.com

Dale of Norway
4750 Shelburne Road
Shelburne, VT 05482
www.dale.no

Debbie Bliss
Distributed by KFI
www.debbieblissonline.com

Fiber Trends
P.O. Box 7266
E. Wenatchee, WA 98802
www.fibertrends.com

Fiesta Yarns
5401 San Diego NE
Albuquerque, NM 87113
www.fiestayarns.com

Filatura Di Crosa
Distributed By Tahki•Stacy
Charles, Inc.

Gedifra
Distributed by Westminster
Fibers, Inc.

GGH
Distributed by Muench Yarns

The Great Adirondack Yarn
Company
950 County Hwy 126
Amsterdam, NY 12010
www.yarnrep.com

Jade Sapphire Exotic Fibres
866.857.3897
www.jadesapphire.com

KFI
P.O. Box 336
315 Bayview Avenue
Amityville, NY 11701
www.knittingfever.com

Knit One, Crochet Too, Inc.
91 Tandberg Trail, Unit 6
Windham, ME 04062
www.knitonecrochettoo.com

La Lana Wools
136-C Paseo del Pueblo Norte
Taos, NM 87571
www.lalanawools.com

Lane Borgosesia
Distributed by Trendsetter Yarns

Lily Chin Signature Collection
www.lilychinsignaturecollection
.com

Lion Brand Yarn
34 West 15th Street
New York, NY 10011
www.lionbrand.com

Loop-d-Loop by Teva Durham
Distributed by Tahki•Stacy
Charles, Inc.

Muench Yarns, Inc.
1323 Scott Street
Petaluma, CA 94954
www.myyarn.com

Naturally NZ
15 Church Street
Onehunga
Auckland, New Zealand
www.naturallyyarnsnz.com
USA Distributed by Fiber Trends
Canada Distributed by The Old
Mill Knitting Co.

The Old Mill Knitting Co.
P.O. Box 81176
Ancaster, Ontario
Canada L9G 4X2
www.oldmillknitting.com

Plymouth Yarn Company
P.O. Box 28
Bristol, PA 19007
www.plymouthyarn.com

Prism Yarn
www.prismyarn.com

Rowan
Distributed by
Westminster Fibers, Inc.
www.knitrowan.com

UK Green Lane Mill
Holmfirth
HD9 2DX England

Schoolhouse Press
6899 Cary Bluff
Pittsville, WI 54466
www.schoolhousepress.com

Tahki•Stacy Charles, Inc.
70-30 80th Street, Building 36
Ridgewood, NY 11385
www.tahkistacycharles.com

Tahki Yarns
Distributed by Tahki•Stacy
Charles, Inc.

Tilli Tomas
617-524-3330
www.tillitomas.com

Trendsetter Yarns
16745 Saticoy Street, Suite #101
Van Nuys, CA 91406
www.trendsetteryarns.com
Canada
Distributed by The Old Mill
Knitting Company

Unique Kolours, Ltd.
28 N. Bacton Hill Road
Malvern, PA 19355
www.uniquekolours.com

Valley Yarns
Distributed by Webs

Webs
75 Service Center Road
Northampton, MA 01060
www.yarn.com

Westminster Fibers
4 Townsend Avenue, Unit 8
Nashua, NH 03063
www.westminsterfibers.com